Falling For The Win

NFB

<<<>>>

Buffalo, NY

NFB
119 Dorchester Road
Buffalo, NY 14213

For more information visit
Nofrillsbuffalo.com

Falling For The Win

Gary Visconti

Table of Contents

Foreword

1966. Do you remember what the world looked like in 1966? Mutual distrust and dislike, a red under every bed and "better dead than red," culture and sports as tools for demonstrating political superiority, mutually prevailing ignorance and suspicion.

Somehow, common people on both sides of the ocean, at every level, refused to think outside the box and were oblivious to the fact that they enjoy the same emotions, suffer from the same insults and indignities, crave for similar joys, and defend similar values.

Which, by the way, is especially obvious today when we live in a fast expanding worldwide village, with globalizing media and merging cultures! People can order sushi and sake in a Turkish restaurant in New York's Brooklyn, owned by Uzbeks and run by Russians. Or how about a Mexican joint in Alaska run by Chinese? Robert De Niro, who is half Italian and half Albanian, played an American mobster residing in France in a recent movie.

But in '66, in that fast-fading era that eludes our memory, a charming, broadly smiling guy in his early twenties came "To Russia with Love" to win the hearts and minds of thousands of people who welcomed him and his pals and opened their souls to "The Sound of Music" and "West Side Story" and to someone who boldly ventured into their 270 million, ostensibly "unfriendly" land. The hitherto unknown "ping-pong diplomacy," only 10 years earlier.

The globe then was politically split. Politics, stereotypes and bitter distrust cast a gloomy shadow over human destinies in all corners of the globe. The chap from "out there" seemed oblivious of such nonsense and kept smiling at that odd nation, winning friends everywhere he traveled.

Stubborn but caring, insistent and full of ingenuity, broad looking but meticulous in his every step, this guy has been my dear friend for over 47 years. We both have witnessed the collapse of the Berlin Wall, the dismantling of the former Soviet Union and post-war Europe. We both lost friends and close relatives, rejoiced and cried, prevailed and humbled. The world has changed but our friendship survived. And today we both look at this new world with a mixture of pride and amazement: Is it possible that this world started changing way back in '66 and we both contributed, each in his own special way? I know this guy did!

This book reveals the life journey of a man who managed to overcome many adversities, reached for the stars, helped others reach their goals, and paved the way for countless others to follow. Any ethnicity, any culture, any color, any political affiliation — just a human determined to make the world a better place for all.

Thank you, Gary, for being such a great friend! Call me the next time you look for someone to share your crazy ideas with.

— *Vladimir Zvyagin*

Vladimir

An unexpected, "lifelong" close friend.

So while on the World Figure Skating Tour in the winter of 1966, arriving in Moscow, a handsome, well-educated, well-groomed and youngish man was assigned to be my "bodyguard." He spoke better English (American style) than I and was extremely cordial. Peggy Fleming had her confidant and I had mine! He was assigned through the Soviet Sports Bureau. We really hit it off and he traveled with us the entire two-week tour in the U.S.S.R. After regularly corresponding for some 20 years and his occasional work visits to the U.S., Vladimir settled in New York City, becoming the head of the Soviet News Agency, raising three children, and finally a Senior Professor at the Globe Institute of Technology in Manhattan through today.

A lifelong special connection I cherish and respect always.

— Gary Visconti

A Word From the Author

I can't really figure exactly how and why life develops the way it does. It is true that so much of what turns out does depend on decisions we make along the way. But, are those decisions based primarily on experience and intelligence or just self-inflicted, quick responses where we make a choice with our emotions without really thinking it through first? Perhaps our decisions are always a combination of the two or, just maybe, our course is already set before us and it is left to us to choose the path along the way to our ultimate fate and destiny?

My life decisions to ice skate, to drag out college for a skating career, to push myself to my athletic limits, then skate professionally, get married, have children, coach the very top ice athletes in the world, get involved philanthropically, get divorced and even to write this book — did I actually make these decisions deliberately or was it all mapped out for me to follow? I will tell you I had no idea of the significance of the events of my life along the way and I certainly had no idea how important each decision was as it related to my ultimate goals and the eventual outcome of my life.

Sometimes, many times, okay — most of the time — life just happens. Sometimes we just have to go with the flow, not think too much and just naturally respond. Other times, it is so important to stop, look around, listen, and learn about ourselves and from others. What I have learned over the years I would like to now share with you in the pages and chapters of my life that follow. I've learned to try not to judge or criticize myself too much, only learn from an experience no matter how insignificant it may seem. I've learned that lessons come our way every single day if we recognize them. I've learned to keep my eyes open, absorb, learn, experience and grow through it all. Time does not forget, so each little failure (fall) or victory (get-up) is recorded by you in your "life experience file," and we need to call upon that immense file of information to help steer us on the path we have chosen to take.

To choose a life path is not as complicated as you may think. Watch and listen to that which is all around you. Life's "call" — its influence, friends, family, society, geographical location — all play a major roll in influencing you and your decisions. Take it all in and then make your choices. Choose the best life for you then stick to your guns, your goal, your path. As Sir Winston Churchill said: "Never, never, never give up!" What a simple, fantastic motto.

Take this book, for instance. It has been over 10 years since I started to write it and, originally, it was to be for my eyes only. Now here it is, in full view of the whole world. That was not my original goal, it just evolved and I went with it. Opportunity presented itself and I made the decision to go for it. I have never written anything for the public to read and, for most of my life, I never thought I was a smart person or mentally equipped to be a "scholar," let alone a published author trying to share my life-learned lessons.

As a child, life and school were hard for me in the "learning department." Math and science were like Greek to this little Italian boy. And, being left-handed in a Catholic grade school back in those days was viewed as a detriment to learning and something to be corrected by the sisters (think ruler on the knuckles). I always had trouble reading and back then there was no identification of dyslexia or Attention Deficit Disorder (A.D.D.). Looking back, I am sure I was both and still am to this day. I was full of self-doubt as a student but I have never given up and I don't want you to ever give up either — on yourself or your dreams.

What I really want to share with you is … everything I have learned through living. Oh, not so much about sports in general or even figure skating, specifically, but about life; about finding your place in life, and about observations and inspirations that lifted me up along the way. I want to share with you and encourage you to find out what you love in life and then how to go for it, not holding back but pushing yourself without fear of failure or even of success. I want to inspire you to dream first and then make it happen — for you!

We're all in this together, each with special gifts and something unique to offer. What is common among us are the stages of life we all work our way through from planning (dreaming) to competing (participating in life) to fulfillment (potential realized) to love and sharing and teaching and, of course, giving back. The perfect seven — decades of our lives in which, ultimately all seven come together continually to form that never-ending circle in every day, every decade, every phase of our life no matter our age or where we come from or our circumstance. There is definitely something to be said for identifying, defining, and then living each stage of our life to its fullest … and I want to say it and share it and examine it along with you. So this is my story written in my words, by me for you!

Join me, please, as I take you through the adventure of my life that has been blessed with so many special people and places and experiences, wonderful rewards and memories made. And hopefully, along the way, you will see part of yourself in me — the struggle, the successes, the failings but always, in the end, the dusting yourself off and the getting back up again. I call it, Falling for the Win.

Acknowledgements and Dedication

Thankfully, there have been special people along the way to help encourage me and guide me to my better self. One was my high school drama teacher, Rosemary Kluffman, who I remained friends with until her passing in 2007. What a super great lady. She and her sister flew to New York City for my American professional skating debut at Madison Square Garden. She was the Drama Department at Osborn High and really for the entire East Side of Detroit. I was also positively influenced by two uncles who were both automotive designers and always encouraged me to pursue my art and to draw and paint and explore whatever creative side was in me. There were also a few great competitors along the way who gave me the drive and challenged me to succeed.

In the pages that follow you will read much about the only coach in my life, Mr. Don Stewart, and how he took me, literally, from a little no-name skater in East Detroit to points around the world I never learned about in school. He saw something in me and helped to bring that out in a way, on an icy venue, so that I could share it with the world!

My Mom was always there for me and my skating, helping me to live a life she herself could only dream of. And there was Dad, perhaps the single biggest contributor to my character. You know, I think the greatest thing he taught me was to learn how to do something and then creatively get it done! Mom always wanted things improved around the house and, in time, we needed to expand the little two-bedroom house we called home. So Dad, after a long day at work, would come home, eat supper, and then "get to it" fixing and building and creating more space for us — fantastic! His work ethic was unmatched and I learned so much from watching and helping him.

I want to thank Dr. Patti Donze for her encouragement and guidance and Joe Kirchmyer for his expertise in helping launch this book.

And then there was you, maybe a fan of my skating in the past or just an interested new reader into my life. You have been there for me, then and now, and I dedicate this book to you ... that all I have been through in the past may help you on your present journey. I also dedicate myself, and all that I hope to be moving forward, to helping you find your best path in life and reach your potential.

Introduction

I started skating at 40. Still recuperating from a bad car-versus-bicycle accident from law school, centering my weight on the blade helped me to center myself. Often the only adult in a rink full of 12-year-olds, in all the fantastic dorkitude of beginning adult skating ... it was Gary that made really made me feel welcome and at home. Sure, initially it was just familiarizing me with the oddities of skating, but Gary also helped me to realize that I had already found my place in the world. With all the bumps in the road I hadn't noticed how important I was to my own students. Thanks, Gary, for showing me that.

I started working with Gary at a challenging time in both of our lives. For Gary, his father had just passed and he was contemplating retirement. During our lessons, sometimes I would skate back over to find him reliving relationships with important father figures or contemplating issues of identity. This is where his mind went. He told me once that he felt really vulnerable and he wasn't used to feeling that way. I had gotten used to it and it was easy for me to help him be comfortable with that feeling, too. Then he returned the favor. I learned so much about what it takes to pick yourself back up again by watching him do just that. I really thank the universe for sending me Gary when she did because he modeled for me how to heal yourself. We both learned a lot from each other and it has resulted in a strong bond of friendship that makes Gary forever family to me. Coaches really are the true heroes.

This book is about what it takes to pick yourself up, keep going, and succeed. In today's world where the gap between rich and poor seems to grow every minute, it is easy to think that life's rewards go to only a few. Certainly this is true in skating, where so few people achieve those coveted national and international titles. But the message of this book is that everyone has what it takes to lead a successful life. The book is called Falling for the Win because, as Gary says, "Losing creates a resiliency in you that you will need many times over in the future." Contrary to what many believe, it is not talent that makes us successful. Everyone is a genius in their own way, with talent waiting to be discovered and nurtured. It is how we respond to the challenges in our lives that makes us role models to the next generation.

Gary has learned a lot about what it takes to be successful in life. I hope that you, the reader, can learn from Gary in the same way that I learned from him as his student.

— Dr. P. Donze, PhD

Los Angeles, 2014

Decade 1: Planning

Dream, Dream, Dream ... Then Achieve!

Plan: a: method for achieving an end b: an often customary method of doing something c: Procedure: a detailed formulation of a program of action d: Goal, Aim: an orderly arrangement of parts of an overall design or objective: a detailed program
— Webster's Dictionary

Planning ... at this early stage in life, we call it "kid dreaming." But, dreams are real inner motivational thoughts and are ignited by your own personal fate. A dream, or plan, is a self-initiated fate, a gut feeling toward your chosen destiny.
— Gary Visconti

What You Can Imagine You Can Create

- A "Garyism"

East Detroit, 1956 ... winter ... five degrees above or below zero ... can't really remember. Does it matter? Between Seven Mile and Eight Mile roads just off of Hoover Road in a lower income neighborhood (the one rapper Eminem popularized in his 1997 8 Mile movie — you get the picture). The Fire Department had just flooded the center of Calimera Park for ice skating and on that cold, frosty November morning after finishing my sixth grade homework, I begged my Mom to let me go out and skate before it got dark. My window of opportunity was narrowing as the street lights turned on at precisely 4:50, a kind of first warning, and I absolutely had to be home by 6 p.m. sharp to greet my father for family dinner. Dinner was a very important time at the Visconti household in those days as there were five of us and we were each given 10 minutes after we finished dinner to tell the others what we had done that day. I hoped to tell the others about my time ice skating if Mom would let me go. I was even willing to forego watching the Flash Gordon and Howdy Dowdy TV shows if she would say yes!

Detroit can be a bitter cold place in the winter. I can remember snow drifts four to five feet high in front of our garage door. When I wanted to skate on the pond at the park, I had to shovel it. I really enjoyed and "respected" the ice when I had to take 30 minutes to clean the snow off! Then the older boys would come and bring their hockey sticks and pucks and take over the pond. After a lot of negotiation, I would "acquire" a small section of ice where I could safely practice my crossovers and one-foot glides, occasionally jumping and hopping over flying pucks and profanity flung my way. The guys were older and bigger than me but I could move much faster. The big gamble each "skate night" was to be home before 6 p.m. for dinner. I made a pact with my younger sister, Debby, that if I wasn't home by 6 p.m. she would run over to the park and call for me. Usually, she saved me from getting into trouble ... more times than I can share, for sure.

Willpower Is Governed By Will

On Friday and Saturday, I could skate on the pond all day until 9 p.m. That was a treat; extra skate time after dinner if the weather permitted. I would skate until my mother would literally become concerned about me freezing. I was more worried, on the other hand, about those hockey-playing block bullies mocking me and calling me "Sonja Henie" as they skated around me, slapping the puck at me. But I was always quicker and more clever than they were, in my size nine figure skates (I was actually a size six but, in those days, you took whatever skates were available to you and you made it work). I loved the feeling of gliding fast over the white surface of the ice, wind in my face and bullies in my rear view mirror! They literally kept me on my toes. Once in a while, my Aunt Jenny and I would go to Lake St. Clair and skate for hours (and miles), but only on those days when Mother Nature cooperated and made conditions just perfect. Aunt Jenny was a lot of fun, always ready for the unusual and never afraid to try, or say, anything. She always encouraged me to skate, and I did whenever I could! I love her for that till this day.

No Ceilings

Looking back, entertaining was somehow in my bloodstream, a flowing fate that coursed through me and I honestly don't know where it came from. I tried tap dancing at age eight or nine, loved it, but was only okay at it (it didn't seem challenging enough for me). We didn't have Dancing With the Stars or So You Think You Can Dance or America's Got Talent so I didn't really see any future in dancing though my sister Debby and I did get on a local rock 'n roll dance hour on TV (WXYZ Detroit) called The Ed McKinzey Show. It was a spinoff of the American Bandstand Dick Clark production. Debby was eight and I was about 11 and we had a blast dancing the "Chicken" to Bill Haley and the Comet's "Rock Around the Clock." The next year we did it on ice, at Mr. Don's Spring Ice Show at the Ice Flair Rink. Debby couldn't skate at all so we had to push her out on the ice to set up for the number. In my passion to perform I even put on talent shows, using our garage as the theatre and making my Mom sit and watch the productions that I starred in; very versatile numbers, if I do say so myself, with records playing and everything.

But one day while watching TV, I saw Barbara Ann Scott, Canadian, World, and Olympic Champion, on one of the variety shows. Wow — a show and a sport all in one and an individual sport, to boot, where you could be the star! I thought to myself, "That is for me!" I was 9-1/2 years old and my Dad thought I was nuts and was very skeptical of the whole idea of figure skating. But, I had found what might work for me and I stayed with my gut for two long years, begging and pleading to start ice skating — somehow!

Navigate Your Own Road To Happiness

I loved skating so much, in fact, that I had begun to beg my mother to take me to an actual ice rink and, get this, maybe even have a lesson or two. Now, lessons were not cheap in those days as it cost something like $2.50 for each 30-minute private lesson. But ever since watching Barbara Ann Scott on the Colgate Comedy Hour on our little black-and-white TV (Barbara had won the Ice Queen Crown in the Olympics), I knew that I wanted to glide and float and fly across the ice like she did. So, one Saturday my mother took me to the Michigan State Fair Public Ice Rink and let me skate all day for the admission price of $1.00. I believe it was the second Saturday of skating my heart out all over that public rink that Sue Snyder, the skating instructor there, took notice of me and came over to suggest to my mother and I that I take lessons (apparently she saw something inherent in my abilities that I had only felt inside of me but didn't realize it was showing). Yes! It was just what I needed, an ally in my thirst for skating knowledge. I had three lessons over the next four weeks after which Ms. Sue proclaimed that I had successfully learned everything that she could possibly teach me and passed me along to a rink and an instructor in Grosse Pointe.

The First Step Toward A Goal Is The Most Important One Of Many

That night, Mom and I went home to Dad and excitedly told him what the instructor had said. Let's just say that he was less excited than we were about the possibilities. Dad was skeptical, and that was even before we told him that the lessons were to be given way over in Grosse Pointe! Dad turned red and began grumbling something about how that was the wealthiest community in the Detroit area. Money and distance were not the only obstacles in play. Dad was a natural athlete and a very well-known local amateur baseball player, but he knew nothing about figure skating. It took four weeks of my begging and Mom working him over, no doubt, during which time I would take the bus to the State Fair Grounds Rink and practice on my own. Then, the fifth Saturday, my Mom called out to me, "Let's go skating, Butch" ("Butch" was my Mom's nickname for me) and off we went to Grosse

Pointe. I was 11-1/2 years old and on my way! Of course, I didn't really know where I was going or how to get there, so I very blindly left my fate in the hands of others, trusting them to take me where I couldn't go myself. All I knew, in my soul, was that I loved — truly loved — to skate and perform. Mom always knew that and created a "life support" to my dream.

Life Is A Gift; What You Choose To Do With It Is Your Choice

Mom was always up for an adventure, and boy did she know how to dress for the occasion. "Putting on the dog" was the term for it back in the day, I believe. And she looked like a million dollars in her bargain basement dress and costume jewelry as we headed out for the wealthy side of town. Dad said that she really knew how to play the role, and I can remember that she did know how to strut her stuff and play the role of the Grosse Pointe matron as we strolled into the rink that had been converted from an old movie theater called the "Ice Flair." The part-time manager, also to be my coach, was Donald Stewart, a tall, athletic, 26-year-old who had all of the good looks of a movie star. I, on the other hand, must have looked pretty ridiculous to him in my three-sizes-too-big skates protruding from my short self and skinny limbs. But, my little reputation had preceded me thanks to Sue Snyder. Mr. Don (as Mr. Stewart insisted on being called) agreed to take me on as a student provided that we buy a pair of brand new skates for me — a pair that actually fit! Well now, this would be a problem as the price tag attached to that purchase was something like $30.00, and on top of the $5.00 per lesson fee and the trips all the way across town, how were we going to make it work? And, who exactly was going to tell Dad? Mom and I would have to strategize on this one, but exactly how would prove to be a challenge.

A "Handicap" Can Embellish A Person's Desire To Succeed

So many dreams die right about here you know, the point where hopes are dashed right smack into the brick wall of reality. My Uncle Leo, Aunt Jennie's husband, and Uncle Pat were so cool, they had it all – loud jazz, and both progressive automotive auto designers, one at Ford Motor Company and one at Chrysler. I wanted to be just like them. Of course, my new passion was ice skating. Maybe I can do both? They really advised me not to be a car designer. They said that someday machines will do the designing, not artists. I listened to them and started drawing just for fun.

Dad was a welder/engineer at Ford making $105.00 a week and his one release, his passionate hobby, was as a semi-pro bowler, an activity that cost him $15.00 a week. So how were we going to afford to pay for my new hobby and was that going to mean that Dad was going to be asked to give up his? Mom knew what I didn't ... that Mr. Don, after watching me skate, was really interested in taking me on and teaching me all he knew. But another reality that she also knew was that he already had a student who not only was further along and could do spins and jumps but also came from a well-to-do Grosse Pointe family who could, no doubt, afford many lessons. This was neither going to be an easy decision nor a small thing to pull off. This was going to be a family decision, a family commitment, a change of priorities and lifestyle, and expensive, too! Everyone would be affected and feel the squeeze.

UNITED STATES FIGURE SKATING ASSOCIATION

30 HUNTINGTON AVE., BOSTON, MASS.

1956-1957

This Certifies that ___Gary Visconti___

of the ___Individual Member___

IS REGISTERED BY THE ASSOCIATION

Secretary

N? 159

My United States Figure Skating Association ID Card.

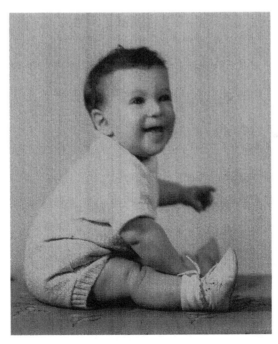

Me at 18 months.

My very first competition.

Jimmy Savitas, Mr. Don Stewart and me.

Me, Sandy Shaw and Dougie Ramsey at a Skating Club Show in 1958.

Mom and Dad 'Cutting a Rug'.

My older sister, Judy, was already in her second year of high school, a cheerleader and quite the social butterfly. I could only imagine at the time, as her little 11-year-old brother, what it might mean to her blossoming and burgeoning status as one of 7 Mile's most popular teenagers to have to tighten the purse strings?

My little sister, Debby, was a tomboy and had just begun playing baseball. Mom, while a very creative shopper, did like to spend money and was directly at odds with Dad who, by nature, was very, very frugal and conservative. Together they made a good team, agreeing to play it safe and not take any chances like moving or changing jobs so that we kids would have a very safe, predictable, almost Leave It to Beaver upbringing. But money always was a challenge and, let's say, a topic of discussion in the Visconti home.

I remember one Friday evening when Dad got home at 6:15, right on time, just like clockwork, and had his cash in hand having taken his $105.00 paycheck to the bank on his lunch hour. Anyway, Mom had the large payment envelope all ready to go with slots for the electric bill, phone bill, mortgage, food, etc. The deal was — the ritual was — to slot and store away money from each week's check so that by month's end, or beginning, there would be all the necessary money there for all the necessary bills.

Dreaming, Alone, Does Not Create Results

The only money slot Mom could play with or borrow from (in her mind), in case of an emergency or an extreme "want" or "need," was the food slot. And truth be told, the Visconti household was very blessed through the years in terms of little to no emergencies but definitely, occasionally, some very real "wants" and "needs" on the part of mother. It was common knowledge, an open family secret, that when Mom wanted something extra we would all get something much less desirable to eat that week. Like the time Deb wanted a new green parka jacket ... I think we had cream tuna on toast three times that week as Mom dipped into the food fund (I remember Dad calling it "shit on a shingle"). Then there was the time Mom was sick and tired of the old furniture and vowed to correct that little bit of a homemaking oversight. Well, we must have had chipped beef and peas on toast till we were all peeing green because I remember Dad getting so mad when the furniture arrived that he had it all sent back and we sat without furniture for months on end as neither of our parents would give in to the other's point of view. Usually, in the end, Dad would work out a truce and all would be settled (exactly as Mom had intended). Mom really knew how to deal with Dad and get him to see things in a new light — her light. Wow, the power of women.

A Sacrifice For A Goal Is No Sacrifice At All ... It Is The Pathway To Reward

In the end, after a family discussion, everyone agreed to support my dream and do what it took to make my lessons happen. It was truly a family decision brokered by Mom. Certainly I was overjoyed but the impact of that decision, in those days, has only been fully realized and appreciated by me after all these years. What a family; I was truly blessed.

And as an example of divine principle or, at the very least, good karma, let me tell you what happened in the weeks and months that followed. Dad continued his bowling and actually started producing winnings, enough that he often could afford to pay for my lessons straight out of his bowling purse. And then on St. Patrick's Day, 1956, while I was already skating now three times a week (in only my third week of skating), I showed up to skate with green dyed hair — and that was not the biggest surprise of the day. Mr. Don, who was scheduled to return to the professional ice show "Hollywood Ice Revue" starring, of all people, Sonja Henie, decided to accept a full-time manager/teacher position at the rink. But, here is the kicker. In doing so he also talked the owner, Mr. Toni Lido, into giving me free practice ice time! Do things sometimes work out or what? True, earlier in the day I was sent home early from school by Sister Laura to try and wash some of that green dye out of my hair but, in the end, that is a day I will never forget ... and neither will St. Raymond's School.

"Growing Up" In A Strange New World

That Summer of '56, I was 12 years old and eating up every bit of coaching Mr. Don could possibly throw my way. Like a dried up sponge, I absorbed every word of instruction. When coach decided to take a long summer vacation he sent me to Cobourg, Ontario, Canada to train with his old friend Don Tobin. I was put up with a couple who were friends of Mr. Tobin for six weeks and, although the wife was very warm and loving, the couple sure did fight a lot. I wasn't used to such behavior as this kind of open display of hostility did not exist in my house or, at least, wasn't visible to us kids. Sure, Dad was kind of old school and strict but we all knew that Mom really ran the household and together they had either agreed early on in the marriage or forged

33

through the years a peaceful environment in which to raise their family. To be in a non-Catholic household with a stressed out fighting couple all summer long was certainly a new experience for me.

I later found out that Mr. Don's extended vacation had everything to do with his own marital problems and ultimate divorce after only two years of marriage (he and his wife had met and fallen in love while performing in an ice show, and she was now living in New York). Subconsciously, I think I was less ready to grow up and be thrown into adulthood after that summer, I'll tell you. I saw and learned a lot on how not to act as an adult in a relationship. As a 12-year-old, I did not understand the dynamics between couples and I only knew my parents' relationship. This stress was new to me and I was forced to watch and learn another side of couples' relationships.

"Quest" ... To Go After Something With A Positive Approach

But, overall, my Canadian skating adventure with Mr. Tobin was a special interlude in my life. Little did I know that Mr. Don had sent me up there with a long-range plan in mind. At the end of my six-week tutelage, my parents came to visit me and Mr. Tobin tried to convince them to let me stay longer and train with him. Boy, was Mr. Don mad when he heard that. You see, he had it in mind all along to have me ready to compete at the Juvenile level in the States the following January. In order to qualify, I had to pass two figure tests. While training with Mr. Tobin, I barely passed my first figure test and then Mr. Don was going to take me through figure test number two and away we would go to the Juvenile competition. I didn't realize at the time that I was being "fought" over by two very good coaches and that was probably just as well for the moment as it kept my little 12-year-old head the proper, approximate size that a humble 12-year-old's head should be. Visiting and training up in Canada for most of the summer was enough for this sheltered Italian Catholic boy who, for the first time, was living away from home by himself with strangers. I was 400 miles away from home but doing what I loved to do, at all costs, sacrificing the security of a loving home and learning about other family life.

One year after my very first lesson, I was competing in the 1957 Midwestern Sectional Juvenile Championships in Sioux City, Iowa. What a rush! I finished second to Bobby McKay who was at the event for the third time. To finish second in a field of 16 competitors from 12 states in my first competition ... well, the die was cast and I was on my way! Later, in April, in a field of 13 boys, I won the Niagara Invitational in Buffalo, New York, and that mark was really visible now in the form of a bull's eye on my back. I was the target of the next class of up and coming boy skaters. Mr. Don was now in full control of my every move, test and show and had me on the ice six days a week, three to four hours a day. All of my practice sessions (ice times) were free at this point and Mr. Don made sure that my private lesson fee never exceeded $15.00 a week, no matter how much he instructed me, and believe me I truly needed constant strong and driven coaching.

To Make Your Mark, You Must Take Aim

In those days, competitive figure skating included a series of eight figure tests and three free-skating tests which, when passed, qualified a skater for specific levels. Usually, it would take eight long

plete them all. When I began skating, most of my future

had already been skating for four years. So, Mr. Don's plan

to push through all eight tests in just four years and became

an elite skater — an almost impossible task. I was certainly up for it but

had no idea of the political nature of figure skating in that day and the

plan was nearly sidetracked by the local skating club officials and

judges who would oversee the testing process. Long story short, there

unfolded a "drama" staged by some of the local club officials as to

whether a little Italian Catholic boy from the wrong side of town could

or even should join the private, elitist Detroit Figure Skating Club

(membership of almost $1,000.00 a year) in order to represent my

region in competitions around the states. I wish people were never

considered for membership in those early days. Who was this little

upstart kid who didn't even practice at the club but instead practiced at

the crummy old rink across town under the inexperienced eye of that

"no-nothing ice show coach?"

The Other Side Of The Tracks

Fortunately, Mr. Don had a long-time friend who was a

member of that stuffy club, Mr. Bill Martin, who sat on the Board of

Directors, and the first giant obstacle of sponsorship into the club was

hurdled. Of course, getting in did not mean that I was "accepted." But

again, there was one special guy who came to my rescue — a quiet

skater of my same age (as it turned out, our birthdays were only days

apart) who was very, very good! Doug Ramsey was the skater in our

age bracket and he knew everyone at the club, including all the rich,

spoiled brats, and they all loved him. I don't know how things would have turned out for me in that setting at that time had it r

Doug, but I never had to find out. He became my very be.

skating brother. He, too, trained most of the time at a different i.

knew how I sometimes felt left out and how I had to deal with

comments about my coach not being a "club" staff coach.

Choose Wisely Your Goals And Carefully Your Companions

Decade 2: Competing

compete: to strive consciously or unconsciously for an objective (as position, profit, or a prize) ... to be in a state of rivalry <competing teams>
— Webster's Dictionary

Competing ... Many obstacles come along the way on the road to achieving your goals. You are challenged, and rightly so, to earn your dream, your goal, your destiny. "Earning your way" ultimately means more and carries with it a sense of fulfillment. Compete daily with honor, inner strength, and focus towards completion. Never give up!
— Gary Visconti

"Winning" and "losing" are funny things. I only realized the past few years that I had competed only 33 times in my entire career. I had won first place 11 times, second place 11 times, and third to sixth place 11 times – weird! But I guess winning one-third of your competitions, and a silver medal in another third, is quite a victory. I am sure, though, that I have lost several times when I should not have — and maybe won gold a few times when I probably should not have.

One big factor stands out after all that: I only really learned when I lost. Losing is a great "lesson" experience and gives you the kick in the butt to wake up and see what and how you can improve on that which is already "top drawer." And on the ice, as in life, one key factor about putting yourself out there and your talents on the line in competition is that it creates a resiliency in you that you will need many times over in the future. Competing in life truly does yield its own rewards and is worth every bit of blood, sweat, and heartache that it delivers. The investment in you and your talents is worth it — trust me.

The Journey Toward A Goal Is More Rewarding Than The End

When I first started ice skating as a boy, I never really knew there were "competitions." I had no exposure to the Olympics or anything of that sort, and skating championships were not on television. Winning or beating someone out for first place was kind of a foreign concept to me. My motivation was the pure challenge of the sport and the learning of it. I enjoyed performing and the whole activity was interesting to me. Such is the pure heart of all of us when we are young.

Today everything is all about the gold, gold, gold.

After a while spent on the ice I wanted to become the best skater in the whole world, but I didn't know how to do that. The whole art of skating, flying through the air and the double and triple turns seemed like magic to me — far away, dreamy magic. I had only been skating 14 months when Mr. Don took me to the Nichols School Rink in Buffalo. It was to be my first international competition and 12 other boys were entered into the contest. They were from Canada and the U.S.

Boy, was I surprised when I won! I came in first place in both figures and freestyle. That was my first taste of winning. Good thing that, at age 12, I didn't realize what a hard path I had chosen to follow and all the difficulties that were waiting for me down the road. But blindly working toward my goal was a good thing and I may never have arrived at my ultimate destination if not for the steady, faithful, unquestioning commitment I had to my dream and coach.

Only my coach had the vision and foresight to push me forward and keep me on the fast track up the competitive ladder. I totally believed in his vision using my desire and I let him take control of the process; I just wanted to be really good! Mr. Don was a driven man. I think he was always trying to prove to himself and to the world, "I can make it." I felt partially for me and my career, but for him, too. It seemed he was never validated by his father and was constantly trying to prove his worth.

After he left the "Ice Flair," he and his ice show friends, Ron and Audry Brown, opened their own ice skating studio rink similar to a small dance studio. Not a full ice rink, and at that time from 1960 to 1965 they were the instructional rage in the Midwest. Mr. Don and Ron expanded to two studios, then after 2-1/2 years opened a full-size ice arena called "Iceland" in Troy, Michigan. All during this time I trained on the small 40'x 60' ice studio housed in a storefront building in Berkley, Michigan. This environment made for quick, compact and exact skating as there was no room for error! It especially helped in the figure eight category. I did go to various NHL hockey size rinks to lay out and train for my freestyle routines. The Detroit Skating Club was my home base for this, and at that time open October through May and housed in an old equestrian barn that was not insulated and sometimes only 14 degrees inside. Practicing without Mr. Don was a great act of self-discipline but also had its challenges not having a "club pro" watching out for me. Dougie and I had shared this feeling daily as he also trained in a studio environment.

Eventually, Ron and Mr. Don split and Mr. Don went on staff at Michigan State University and I moved up to East Lansing to live and train with him in 1964 and stayed until 1969, and attended classes at the university.

My next big competition was the 1958 Novice Level Nationals in Rochester, New York, which I qualified for through the Midwestern Championships. I won the free skating portion but, due to low figure placement (fifth) in the technical portion of the competition, I finished well out of first place at my first nationals. Still, I did get to show off my natural skating ability and Mr. Don's plan for my future remained in full swing.

That summer (of '58), Mr. Don arranged for me to skate at Michigan State University Arena some 90 miles away, because he took his long summer break. I loved the fact that Dougie, my new friend, would be there and that I would be coached by his coach, Mr. Bill Swallender. To boot, we were joined that summer by the likes of three-time World Champion Carol Heiss, Canadian champion Don Jackson, the Jelenicks (world pair skaters), all students of Mr. Brunet, and National Junior champion Bradley Lord and National Novice champion Greg Kelley. I hung out with them in the skaters' dorm (Gilchrest Hall) and trained side by side on the ice. I watched and listened and I grew in my sport — what an advantage! We had weekly ice shows on Saturday nights and those experiences helped me mature as a performer and competitor.

Thanks to Mr. Don, I was surrounded by some of the best skaters in the world and I don't think it was any coincidence at all that

'58 was the year that my skating ability took a quantum leap (so to speak)! Mr. Pierre Brunet, world coach, first noticed and liked me that summer. What a great Frenchman he was, the former World Pair Champion and always a true gentleman. Later in our friendship he took me to his beautiful cabin in Boyne City, Michigan, where I spent a great week with him and his wife Andre. There he introduced me to antiquing, and I started collecting spittoons and I still do to this day.

As I headed into public high school (ninth grade) after completing all of my elementary years in the care of the nuns at St. Raymond's, I was both apprehensive and excited for my future prospects both on and off the ice.

The First Step Is Usually The Hardest

January of 1959 saw me qualify for the Novice Nationals and I would love to tell you that I dominated the competition and took another major step in my development but a strange thing happened instead on my way to stardom — it took longer than we thought. You know how it is when you've been successful one time and you worry about that next outcome? Well, I was totally freaked out by everyone's expectations for me to win the Novice title. And, combined with my own expectations of living up to the legacy of my superhero David Jenkins, who was National Champion and a World Champion, looking back I think I was a little bit afraid of success and held back. Mr. Don, who had pushed me so fast and so hard, also pulled back the reigns a little — a philosophy we would not employ again in the future. And, I went through a natural growth spurt and became an awkward 14-year-old. Altogether, I guess you can only push Mother Nature and maturity so far and, combined with the new jumps and challenging programs at this next level, I didn't even medal that year.

Find Time Not Relative To Success

But, when you are sincerely trying your best and moving forward, even when stumbling, good things usually happen to those who persevere. At the very least, failure brings about change which can then lead to a better road ahead. The biggest change for my coach and I in our skating strategy came with the realization that maybe Mr. Don had let me skate too much on my own, and he was going to rectify that himself. That summer of '59, Mr. Don and I trained together in Cleveland, Ohio — six to seven hours a day! Hands-on training, move for move, personal instruction at its most intense. Don rented a big house in Shaker Heights and Mom came along to be a "den mother," of sorts, to 10 kids and three adults. Between cooking and cleaning, kids breaking arms and my own poison ivy, well, Mom was busier than sin. She was always so upbeat and funny and nurturing. On top of everything going on there in Cleveland, Mom became a grandmother and I became an uncle as my oldest sis, Judy, became a mother at age 19. We were so happy and proud of her and her husband.

The Road Of Life Has No Maps – Create Your Own Path

(The Training Wheels Come Off)

Training was much more interesting, personal, and intense for me that summer of 1959 as Mr. Don pushed me and himself past obstacles and through barriers that I did not even know were there previously. There were tests and ice shows and, all the time, there was Mom — right there by my side. I was sharing time, training and teenage fun with my skating brother Dana Charette that summer, and it was great. I exchanged letters with Dougie, who was skating at the Michigan State facility again that summer, and we were both working hard towards the Junior level competitions.

I, ultimately, had trouble passing all of my tests that year to reach the Junior level (those credentials would come easily to me the next year), but what I remember most about the next step of my journey between the Novice and Junior levels of my sport was being aware and watching the 1960 Squaw Valley Winter Olympic Games. After my first competition, every year I competed I qualified for the U.S. National Team, whether it was Novice, Junior, or Senior, except for this one year — 1960. This would have been my third Nationals and I missed qualifying by one placement out of the Midwest Championships. It was an Olympic year, too, and I had so been wanting to see all the great ones perform: Carol Heiss and David Jenkins and all the Nationals getting ready for the Games in four weeks. I was totally devastated in the weeks leading up to the Squaw Valley Olympics (my first real awareness and exposure to the Winter Olympics). To make matters worse, the Games were so close, in California, yet so far away and I didn't really have any "ways and means" to get there. But, I did promise myself that soon, very soon, I would be there and not just as a spectator but as a competitor! I would one day be an Olympic athlete representing my great country, the U.S.A., in the most glorious sport of all performing on the ice as America's top figure skater — God willing!

Just about now, in 1959, Dad was offered a great promotion with the Ford Motor Company — the company he had been affiliated with since 1932 in the trade school — to a high position in Brazil, South America. After many long family discussions and me (at 14) encouraging him to accept, and I would stay in Michigan to skate and live with Mr. Don and his mom, Dad said "No, I want my family to always be together." I think he should have taken the position as I am sure it wasn't forever. He was always thinking of us first.

Success Is Perceived By You

Later that year I did qualify for Juniors through my testing and, in fact, at 1961 Sectionals that year I skated the Senior Men's Event which was customary back then! Of course, even if I somehow miraculously won this competition I would still only skate as a Junior at the 1961 Nationals. On the other hand, if I could somehow finish in the top three among those competitors above me it would mean an automatic qualification for me at Junior Nationals. Well, I did it and qualified for the National Championship! It was a long-shot and I ended up fifth at the Junior National competition but it boosted my confidence and "stretched" my perception of what I was capable of doing.

Strength Of Character Is Slowly Developed And Constantly Challenged
Teenage Tragedy – Never Forget …

Of course, nothing could have ever "stretched" my perceptions of reality, of expectations, of the world around me and my place in it like the events of February 1961. I had just qualified for Junior Nationals and finished in fifth place in the Colorado Springs, Colorado, competition. Mr. Don was not pleased with the scoring that had placed me out of the top three but the harder news to take was Dougie's fourth place finish in the Senior Men's Division, just missing out on a place on the World Team by one spot! He was named first alternate for the World Team. Can you imagine, at Doug's age, our age, representing the country at international events? We were all happy. How cool and exciting.

The week after we got home from the Colorado U.S. Nationals, Tim Brown, number three in America, fell ill and retired from skating. As fate would have it, Dougie was put on the team going to the 1961 North American Championships in Philly and then named on the U.S. World Team. We had a huge "bon voyage" party for him at the club. Our boy had made it! A few days later he would leave for the North American Championships in Philadelphia and then onto Prague in the Czech Republic to compete on the world's stage. What an amazing glory; what an experience it would be. I couldn't wait for my friend to return to tell me all about it.

Of course, I followed each day of the entire team's schedule for the next three weeks. I already knew they were all leaving from New York City on Sabena Airlines for Prague, Czechoslovakia, on February 14th, Valentine's Day, just two days after their skate at the American Championships.

On February 15th, at 5:30 a.m., Dad drove me to Don's ice rink, as usual, as I wasn't driving yet. We didn't take his old jalopy car because it was a cold, snowy day in Detroit. We had Mom's newer car and it had a radio. The drive was 45 minutes on a clear day, so we had the news on the radio. And then I heard it. The newsman was so cold and curt. His words cut open my heart.

I remember Dad driving just a little bit fast and sloppy for my taste so when I yelled out, "Oh no!" Dad was no doubt thinking I had spotted something in the road that he did not. "Stop the car, Dad!" I blurted out. "STOP! STOP!"

"Dad, stop the car! Here at the newspaper stand!" I jumped out into the snow and ran back to the newspaper stand we had just passed. Then I thought — NOTHING CAN BE IN THE PAPER YET! IT JUST HAPPENED! So I stumbled my way back into the car, slipping on the wet, sloppy snow and crying.

Dad was very confused with me and asked, "What is it, son?"

"Dad, Dad — they're all dead — all dead," I cried, then through tears I said, "The Sabena plane crashed in Brussels last night and all the kids and coaches are dead. Dead ... all dead!"

Oh my God — Dougie! That was the hell day of my 16th year. It was the worst moment, the worst day of my life. All over the news that day and for days following the reports sounded so, I don't know, cold and matter-of-fact: "On February 15th, 1961, the entire United States Figure Skating Team went down in an airplane crash over the skies of Brussels, Belgium. There were no survivors." I was devastated for days and days and days, and details were so slow and confusing and scary.

Maybe The "Hereafter" Is The "Just Before"

The World Championships were canceled and it would be five weeks of waiting for the bodies to be returned to the States, an eternity of wondering why and how and trying to make any sense out of this seemingly senseless tragedy. To make things worse, Coach Bill Swallender's body came back one week before Doug. So of course we all attended his memorial, and wanted Dougie to come home.

Keep in mind that this was during the height of the Cold War and speculation ran rampant about the possibilities of the plane being shot down or tampered with by the Russians as communications were slow and strained between the U.S. and the Soviet Union. The U.S. was the first country to put out jet passenger planes, and the plane the team was on was new, only on its second trip to Europe. What happened? We never heard the real final and official reason until one year later; of course, the usual "pilot error." These times were strained and communication was slow, secretive and antagonizing between countries.

For weeks and months after the crash, I was numb to the reality of what had happened. Dougie was not only my best friend but my skating idol. It had been my goal to be like him. He was the one I emulated on the ice, that I looked up to, that I owed so much to for making me feel at home in the skating club and within my own potential and possibilities. We could really relate; he was kind and gentle and shyly quiet.

All Of Life Is A Gamble ... But, To Play Is The Real Reward

As one of the pall bearers at Dougie's funeral, some five weeks after his death, I remember carrying the coffin — my first time ever —

and looking at the big steel box. I was startled to find myself in a conversation with him: "Is that really you in there, Dougie? Are all the parts of your body in there with you? The damn plane crashed, Dougie — are you all in there?" It wasn't a rational discussion nor was I in any kind of rational frame of mind to sort out the disaster that had just taken place in the lives of our friends and skating family, in the life of the United States Figure Skating program, in my own life. I could hardly walk let alone carry my friend to his final resting spot.

"Do you know how sad I am that you're gone? We will never skate together again. Who can I talk with about the awkwardness I feel at the club? Who can I hide from, play with, and scare while roaming up in the huge attic of the club?" It used to be The Detroit Equestrian Club years ago and had at least 20 rooms upstairs all abandoned, now only an empty place. "Will your ghost — your soul — roam around in those rooms?" ... rooms now more empty now that he was gone. Do I dare go up there again, ever?

I didn't want to go back to the club after Doug's death; it was eerily empty without my friend. I heard his mother was totally devastated and, after the funeral, I never saw her again. Nothing would ever be the same again for me, I thought, and I was right.

Fate, that strange, ever-turning hand would once again reveal itself to be sardonic, if not twisted, when the entire Junior Figure Skating Team was, all at once, "promoted" to Senior Team status because of the void. Ready or not, all of us Juniors were now Seniors at our regional competitions; 16-year-olds, the lot of us. We were no longer the future of American skating — we were American skating. Just like that, no longer needing to qualify or mature a bit more ... it just was. We were to be the crème de la crème. Not the chosen ones but the ones that were now going to fill their shoes ... a position I never thought I would earn this way.

Destiny Is Written; The Path Is Choice

Life Goes On And On Without Us Or Our Dreams

Motown ... and we are a car family. Dad was with Ford already some 30 years, and even my sister Judy was working there. As a senior at Osborn High School I wanted a car and saved from my part-time job at Green's Artist Supply. I bought a very used 1953 Ford Sedan for $175.00. Yeah, cheap ... and in 1962 gas was like 28 cents a gallon. I had it painted a special dark red at Earl Scheib's for $19.95, put in some store seat covers and blue lights in the front wheel wells and I was the coolest!

In January 1962, as Midwestern Champion, I officially re-qualified for the Nationals in Boston, Massachusetts, as a Junior-level skater. The rules for skating at the Senior National level were that any skater must have placed first, second, or third at the previous National Junior-level competition and must have passed the eighth or Gold level figure test. I was fifth in 1961. Our new 1962 Senior-level skating team was extremely weak and almost void. My figures were great for a change and I was virtually tied with the local favorite, Eastern Champion Tommy Litz, going into the free skate long program. I skated my heart out and everyone, even Tommy and his father, came up to me and Dad afterwards to congratulate me on my freestyle performance and possible win. I had more points in figures and more in the freestyle, but Litz had less ordinals (judges' placement), and less ordinals wins.

What a shock, though, when Tommy was announced as the winner and gold medalist. But, I have to say, winning the silver medal was quite an honor, especially in that year, at that event, where we honored our fallen friends and colleagues. I remember looking around the arena; stark, almost ghastly, in the ominous absence of our deceased Senior skaters. I thought about Tim Brown who had fallen ill and opened up a spot on the team for Dougie, thereby saving himself, in essence, and dooming Dougie to an early grave. I thought about Barbara Ann Roles, the bronze medalist at the 1960 games who had retired early from skating to have a baby — a baby who, for all intents and purposes, saved her life — now here for a comeback and winning the championship of the U.S. to fill a void and to recapture her dream. I tried not to think about my own mortality at a time when so much lie ahead of me, so much promise at such a young age, just like Dougie. I was now looking to the elite Senior National Division next season where so few earned that coveted spot to compete for the top U.S. spot. Last year Dougie only had five men in the elite Senior Division, and he placed fourth ... and this year was worse. Could I do it and make it to the very top, as Dougie would have? Was I worthy of such a task, a goal I could only imagine?

The Human Will Can Be The Single Most Powerful Force In The World

Coaches Are Faceless Heroes

We were all ready to quit the quest.

My first year in the U.S. National Senior Championship was in 1963 in Long Beach, California. It was my first time in California and I reached a remarkable fourth place, unheard of for your first try in a field of 20 of America's best. We were elated by the result. No one there knew I was performing on a severely sprained right ankle. Three weeks earlier during my practice, Mr. Don had me running through my five-minute freestyle routine three times in a row. This technique would build stamina and endurance for an easy "one-time" run of my program. During my third run through I twisted my right ankle on a double lutz takeoff and fell. I went to the doctor's office the next day and he put me on crutches for three weeks and advised no skating for six weeks. I was devastated. I am now the Midwestern Senior Champion and have my place on the national team to compete in my first U.S. Men's National Championship. The Nationals were three weeks away… and what do I do but stay off the ice completely. I did not want to miss my wonderful opportunity to go to California and show my "stuff."

Well, we flew to Long Beach ... my first time on the west coast. I would try to skate the first practice to see how I would do after some 20 days off the ice. There was still pain and luckily Dr. Burhans, the father of our dance team from our rink, was there and said he could help. We needed some luck at this point, so he injected my ankle with cortisone to numb the foot (something we surely didn't want to do, but it was better than the pain or not competing). Our choice was to compete tomorrow, in school figures, on a numb foot. All went great and somehow I won fourth in figures for a real victory, both personal and in that elite group of athletes. The next event, final free skate, was

24 hours later. Another shot, and no pain or feeling whatsoever. Weird ... an ice skater with no feeling in his foot. Wow!

The triple toe-loop was my hardest jump in the opening of my routine; should we do it? Yes or no? Mr. Don said, "Why did we come here? Let's go for it, boy." Well I performed fantastic and became an alternate for the World Team, a real earned honor.

With the impressive showing in California and after the huge awards ceremony, Mr. Pierre Brunet — Olympic and World Pair Champion from France and now an extremely successful coach of World and Olympic Champions and a close friend of Mr. Don's — had a meeting with us. Being internationally connected, he told us of the French Grand Prix Championship that was happening the next month in Megeve, France. He could arrange an invitation for us from France if we wanted it. My coach and I jumped at the chance to compete at an International Grand Prix, and being fourth in the U.S.A., we were sure our Skating Federation would sanction my entry.

A Sacrifice For A Goal Is Not A Sacrifice At All

All worked out and in 23 days we were on our way to Megeve, France, via Paris. This 19-year-old kid from Detroit was going intercontinental. Passport and a jet plane ... the works!

At the time I never was exposed to how this trip to Europe was financed for Mr. Don and myself. Later I found out that Dad somehow paid for it all (I think he got a loan on the house again), even though some of our relatives did offer to help. Love you Mom and Dad; you sacrificed so much for so long and gave so much guidance and strength.

Megeve was high in the French Alps, an outside rink, and I was ready to show my stuff. About 12 countries were represented; three French boys, and I was the only American. Three events: Compulsory jumps and spins, school figures, and the free skate routine. I ranked a perfect second in everything from every judge to one of the very highly favored (you guessed it) French boys. Not like the results were set or anything. A funny thing happened after the awards when a high-ranking French official took Mr. Don and I aside, in a private room, and said, "Gary, you were the best, but you know our French boy must win." Then he gave me a copy of the beautiful first place trophy to take home. It accompanied my silver medal back to Michigan. All in all, we made a great impression! We also learned a great deal about international sport politics.

Now we were off to Paris for three days of a fantastic vacation. One outstanding evening I totally remember is going to see the famous shows at the "Moulin Rouge" and the midnight show at the Lido Club. Well, Mr. Don knew the ice skaters that performed there on the very small piece of 20' x 20' ice, so we had VIP service. After the topless show (which, as a teenager, I was truly blown away) all the showgirls were topless and I must say, I know why! We were invited back stage. I must admit it was one of the first times in my little life that I was in heaven being only 5' 3-3/4" because all the showgirls were very tall, and as we had to pass them in a very narrow hallway I had more than an eye full!

That victory at the Nationals and success in France propelled me into the 1964 skating season, an Olympic Year, and the Nationals were held in Cleveland, Ohio. February in Cleveland was bitter cold outside and intense inside on the ice as the competition level was keen.

We had high expectations and I performed extremely well. This was to be my Olympic bid opportunity. The '63 champion was dethroned and Scott Allen won, Tommy Litz took second and former champ Monty Hoyt — whose Dad owned the Denver Post newspaper — was put down to third (many people in the know said he should have been sixth). Once again, that Visconti character was fourth. Leaving those Olympic Trials (the Nationals) as the alternate was devastating. The bronze had been the goal and I fell just short. We had a big family meeting and Mr. Don felt the National Association let us down big time. Maybe they didn't want us on the team? Maybe we were not what they wanted in a potential champion? So many thoughts and doubts filled my mind. We were all very down and beaten. Going back home empty-handed seemed so shallow. We were ready to stop the quest.

The Biggest Battles Are Fought In Our Minds

Two weeks passed and then the association sent me a formal invitation to go to Germany for the huge International Championships in Garmisch (this became the Junior Worlds). Well, we discussed the invitation for three days and I wanted to do it because after the International Championships we could go up to Dortmund, Germany, and watch the World Senior Championships. Money was very tight and Dad had already mortgaged our home twice to help pay for skating. He quit bowling altogether and used that little money to help pay for lessons and ice time. We paid our own way, and Mr. Don's, too. At that time our skating association did not financially help skaters or international competitions at this level. And all this was a huge strain on the entire family as well as for Mr. Don. I remember him telling me,

"If we go to Germany, you must win!" Okay. No pressure. Yeah, sure. Could I do it?

Keep The Will To Win, The Freedom To Fail

In Garmisch, I skated great school figures and was in first place. The open-air ice stadium was nothing new to me by this time as Mr. Don was training me once a week outside in Michigan from December through February. During our last freestyle practice Mr. Don put a lot of pressure on me to "shape up," as he put it. He said, "The judges are sitting up in the stands at the far end of the arena, pre-judging, and you had better land the triples clean, not under-rotated." I really felt pressured and didn't respond well. He became so upset with me, he said, "Fine, you deal with this final practice on your own!" And he left, still upset. I had a rude awakening that day. He came back to the hotel room five hours later. I told him my run-through went well with both triples. He said, "Fine, tonight you will do all three and win!" Yes, he could push my buttons to overdrive. I realize that's a coach.

The freestyle event went well and, for the first time, I performed three different triple jumps. I received seven first place votes and was in "champion bliss." I was quickly becoming the talk of the European elite judges. They kept asking, "Why was Gary not in Europe before? Where have you been hiding him?" We tried to explain the politics and the difficulty of getting out of the U.S., making the team, and competing through so many skating obstacles there. They told us they heard of my performance last season in Megeve, France, and how I had really "won" the freestyle at the French Grande Prix

Championships. They had been expecting me to be in Europe again, on the team, for the Olympics.

After our win in Garmisch we were flying high on our way to watch the World Championships in Dortmund. We met and mingled with many judges, officials and the ever-so-famous skaters there. It was an experience which changed my skating life and attitude and inspired me to excel even more. I saw great skating and I knew I would be there on that ice next season. Mr. John Shoemaker, the Association president, was so good to me there. I guess they were considering me more of a hot property coming off of my victory in Garmisch. Mr. Don and I were also learning how to play the social game; how to be accessible and interesting to the movers and shakers. We were getting the big picture of international sports and politics.

The German Federation was the real power of skating in Europe and the I.S.U. (International Skating Union) for Figure Skating and Ice Hockey was somewhat controlled by Germany (they had all the World Champions). So the "World Skating Tour" was a huge money maker and Germans ran the entire tour. I was the "German Invitational Champion" from last week so of course they wanted me to go on the tour of 14 cities. Well all hell broke loose among the U.S. team officials because there were only four U.S. skaters allowed on the tour and the U.S. Association was determined to have their champions in those spots. I could not be sanctioned by our association (by their choice) even though Germany wanted me. Competitive opposition was keen, and after all I was only fourth place in America. But watch out next year! Here we come!

Now Mr. Don was ready for a new strategy. That summer's end, 1964, at the Michigan State University arena we set a new

American historical skating record. Remember those very intricate 69 school figures (like piano scales)? Well, I became the first American to take and pass all the International Skating Union figure test standards, thus receiving my third Gold medal for this (like a Ph.D.). Now holding three awards in Canada (1963), U.S.A. (1962) and I.S.U. (1964), we set a new standard and word spread throughout the skating community in the States. Mr. Don always had set goals for me, even in the off season.

We had always felt that our skating spoke for itself and our performance on the ice was ours; for us, first and foremost. We never wanted to owe anyone anything except for respect but, at this level of competition, learning how to interact and present ourselves did not hurt, and listening to the right people would make a difference ... but who were they?

To Run With The Big Boys Takes Fast Feet

The "Ouija Board" predicted it all. At 9 a.m. one Saturday morning at the Detroit Skating Club rink, we were on break in the locker rooms and asking the board to answer our futures ... kid stuff. It was like November around Thanksgiving, 1964. I asked the board, "How will I do at the U.S. Nationals in two months?" It answered: First. We laughed, because I was only fourth best in the U.S.A. then and the current U.S. champ was the '64 Olympic bronze medalist, Scott E. Allen. He was the golden boy. Then a second question by me: "How would I do at the North American Championship if I made it to qualify?" It answered: First. Again, we all laughed. To beat Scott E. Allen, from the Skating Club of New York, and to win over him in his home state, at Lake Placid in the U.S. Championships — then again at the North American Championship in Rochester — would be a miracle. The New York skate club had influence and power back then. But I'll never laugh that way again as it all came true!

Funny, but I still remember for eight months leading up to the January '65 Nationals, that I wanted to do really well. I put an 8 x 10-inch photo of Scott Allen in my skate locker so that every morning at 6:10 a.m. when I opened it to put my skates on for practice I would see his face looking back at me. Boy, did I wake up and get determined to train! Daily and intense — that intense burning desire to succeed.

If You Have To Keep Score, You Are Not "Winning"

1965 — this was the year I bloomed with lots of new experiences and shows and stardom. As U.S. Champion, I was invited to skate for amateur shows all over the nation. Now, if you are a U.S. Champion you can earn one million dollars a year if you are sale-able though endorsements, shows and personal appearances. This is the main reason skaters do not retire from competition; they can pay for their training and make a GOOD living if they are at the top. Since 1992 in the Barcelona, Spain Summer Olympics, the Dream Team of basketball's best competed, so why not all professional athletes? Brian Boitano, U.S. and Olympic Champion, later initiated a huge lawsuit against the International Olympic Committee about this — and won! This opened up the Olympics to all pro athletes.

Now money is an option. In my days amateur meant that you could not receive any gift, or money, or anything over $25 U.S. The association also did not have any money for its elite skaters like it does today. I never, ever received any money to help with my training. My

Dad had to mortgage our little house three times to raise the money for many skating-related things. I remember Harlick Company gave me custom skates several times and I was ever so grateful. All in all it was always a financial struggle and everyone felt the pinch.

To become the champion of America is the dream of every athlete ... number one in the U.S.A. in your sport! Wow, what a huge accomplishment, and to achieve it would be a miracle. What do I have to sacrifice for that goal? Do I have to compromise my beliefs ... follow the crowd ... bow to the puppeteers who would want to pull my marionette strings? Do I give up my family life — Mom and Dad, school, fun, and friends? My art, my passion for perfection in all I try to do? I am 20 years old and trying to find myself as a young man and break away from the huge influence of Coach Don on my every moment for eight years, and also let go of the parent thing (which I did cherish and love and bond to). But it was time to become GARY — whoever he really is! 1965 — The Year of the Visconti!

I had an automatic spot or berth or entry (whatever you want to call it) to go and compete directly into the U.S. top National Senior Men's Championships because the previous year (1964) I was fourth in the U.S. and an Olympic Team and World Team alternate. I was on my way to Lake Placid, New York, to place a respectable and proud second place to Scott E. Allen of New York; he was third at the previous Olympics and the defending U.S. Champion. Mr. Don trained my ass off for six months! It was very intense. He knew this would be tough and my first time to skate, hopefully, at the World scene later that year.

So we are in the 1932 Lake Placid Olympic Arena; wow, what history. The same arena where my earlier namesake Sonja Henie won her second of three Olympic gold medals. What a place, and Scott's home state, too. The evening before we competed Mrs. Allen (Scott's mom) said to my mother up in the stands during our last practice, "Lena, Gary looks good and will be an easy second to my Scottie tomorrow." My mother looked her straight in the eye and said graciously, "Thank you." Later she told us she was ready to slap her! We all laughed and the next day I was in first place in the school figures (they counted for 60 percent of your final score in those days). The following day was only practice before the finals, the five-minute free skate. Everyone gave Mr. Don and my parents congratulations, but a big "but" ... you know Scott will win tomorrow night because that is what the association wants and after all he is third in the world and they are grooming him to win in Colorado Springs at the World Championships next month. I knew the game and the plan, and I have to wait my turn.

We drew for the skating order; Scott drew number 14 and there were only four numbers left in the bag. I put my hand in and prayed to skate last. Number 15 — my prayers were answered! What a showdown this would be! I'll do my best and silver looks real good just about now.

Your Time Is Now

It's Best On Top

This year Mr. Don went all out. He had a new car, a T-Bird. We stayed at the exclusive Lake Placid Club Resort. I have this men's one-piece stretch suit, forest green, very new and edgy for men's competition attire. Mr. Zeno the tailor charged $375, a huge cost for us in those years. We used cool music with quick, light, fast choreography with some unusual elements. Well, Mr. Pierre Brunet (the world class coach) knew skating politics, and he wanted me to win over Scott Allen for many personal reasons. He organized cheering sections consisting of five or six kids all over the arena cheering for me! He really helped control the excitement and atmosphere of the arena that evening.

Scott skated well; not his most exciting performance but he did get the job done. The last skater (me) ... announced from the Detroit Skating Club. Cheers and loud clapping and whistles came from all around the arena before they even said my name. I came out thinking to myself, if I can finish with this applause it would be fantastic. I know I probably would be on the podium with a silver medal and at this time that would be great. I skated light and free and happy, as this was my time. The ice was like soft, oiled glass, fast and free. I finished so quickly that it seemed like only a one-minute show, not the U.S. Nationals. I finished and flew into Mr. Don's big hug on camera with Dick Button calling the shots on ABC's Wide World of Sports, then in its second season on the air.

No computers in those days — scores were held up by hand, right on site, 45 seconds after you finished. My scores were really good from all seven judges. We all ran to figure out the totals by hand and add it to the school figures points. "I think you are first," said Mr. Don, "but let's wait until it is announced." Could it be true?

By now the officials came to the dressing area and asked me to go up to the pressroom, because unofficially I was the new champion! Before the announcement was made to the public, I was rushed upstairs. While walking up, Lee Meade, the Denver Post writer (skating buff) was behind me, and he saw one of the judges, Mrs. Mary L. Wright (who he knew put me in second place by his calculation), and he turned to her and said, "Mary Louise, you would put Jesus Christ second to Scott Allen." She looked so surprised and said, "Well!" I just smiled to myself and went flying into the pressroom. I talked awhile, interviewed and then went down to the ice and stood very tall on the number one spot on the podium. Even on the top step I appeared the shortest but felt nine feet tall.

Upon arriving home three days later there were some 200 congratulatory telegrams, cards, and letters with over 50 more arriving daily. I remember receiving fan mail from Europe, simply addressed:

> Gary Visconti
>
> Ice Skating Champion
>
> Detroit, U.S.A.

Thanks to the U.S. Postal Service, they delivered!

Only two years ago did I find that special box, which Mom had marked "Telegrams for Gary." I must have found 50 or more not even opened yet and had many great moments reading them some 50 years later.

Something Amazing Awaits You — Just Keep Your Eyes Open And Your True Goal Set On The Horizon

After our victory in Lake Placid we drove home to train for the North American Championships three weeks later. Oh boy, here we go again to New York State. Rochester — "Kodak Country" — the home of Mr. F. Ritter Shumway, a huge force in our American Association. I would now face the top Canadian (world experienced) skaters as well as our top U.S. men, again.

I was a dark horse, then a U.S. Champion, and everyone thought it was a fluke. Three weeks later ... North American Champion! Maybe I was top material after all. The United States Figure Skating Association was taking a second look — maybe we had our eggs in the wrong basket, let's look again at the boy from Detroit! In Detroit the newspapers nicknamed me "Zipper" because of how quick I flow over the ice. Quick and fast and happy they said. "A real joy to watch."

As history notes, I was in first place again by a narrow lead in the school figures. The next evening, a big press buildup and the battle for gold between Canadian Champion Donald Knight, Olympic Medalist Scott Allen and me!

I so do remember after our five-minute long program warm-up I was waiting to skate. I became nervously hungry and was in the arena food area in skates (no big security in those days) and ordered a hot dog, not realizing my time to compete was at hand. As they called my name, a UPI (United Press International) press man said, "Gary, if you win now, I'll buy you the dog."

As I went out to set up my start position all I could think about was that hot dog. Well, at evening's end, the win was mine. U.S.A. won three of the four events, and Petra Burka won the ladies along with Peggy Fleming on the podium. I never did receive that hot dog.

The Bigger The Challenge, The Stronger The Effort

The 1962 National Junior Championships... Tommy Litz took first, I claimed second, and Buddy Zack finished third.

I finished first at the 1965 Nationals, with Scott Allen second and Tim Wood third, with John Shoemaker, right, president of the Association.

In 1963, my first European experience in Megeve, France.

The 1966 World podium and third place finish.

Competing figures at The North American Championships.

Competing at the 1966 Nationals.

The outdoor stadium at the 1966 Worlds.

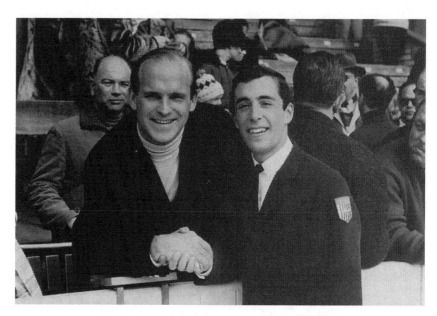

Me and Dick Button at the 1966 Worlds.

With Janet Lynn at the Berlin Wall.

Me and Mom following the medal ceremony at the 1966 Worlds.

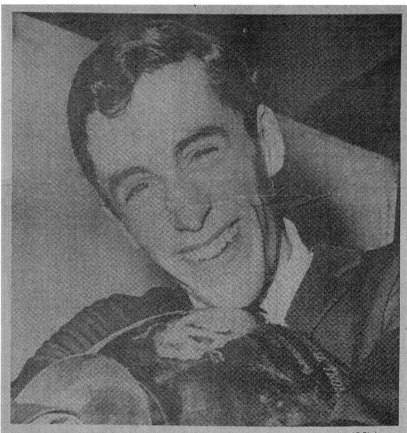

Gary Visconti: The smile of a champion as he hugs his cup

Youth Inspired by Dead Pal Brings Skate Title to City

BY BILL SUDOMIER
Free Press Staff Writer

When it was over, they stood and roared.

When it was over, a whirring top flashed silver across the ice toward a woman at rinkside at the 65th National Figure Skating Championships at Lake Placid, N.Y.

When it was over, the top stopped and Detroit's Gary

"Mama," he said. "I won. I'm champion."

• • •

VISCONTI, 19, of 19500 Fairport, a Macomb Junior College arts freshman, was a champion—at last.

After fourth-place finishes in two straight previous tries for the senior men's title, Visconti made it Saturday. He upset Scott Ethan Allen, 16, of Smoke Rise, N.J. who

The wire service story said two judges voted for Allen and three judges voted for Visconti and added:

" . . . a flawless performance which emphasized steadiness and smooth grace, in favor of twisting spectacular leaps.

For Visconti, it had been a long, long fight.

And it had not been merely

I'm all smiles in this newspaper article.

January 23, 1967

Mr. Gary Visconti
19500 Fairport
Detroit, Michigan 48205

Dear Gary:

     Congratulations on your superlative
victory over the weekend!

     Michigan is, indeed, proud of your
championship achievements which, I know,
reflect years of hard work and desire.

     We'll be watching with great pride
and hope when you compete in Montreal and
Vienna.

     Keep up the beautiful skating.

       Sincerely,

       George Romney

A congratulatory letter from Michigan Gov. George Romney.

Now the real pressure was on. I was to make my first world stage debut and unfortunately for me I had to come in as the American and North American Champion. Wow, what pressure! Now I had Scott Allen behind me. The year before he was 14 years old, third at the Olympics in '64 and the bronze medalist. He was on my heels and both his coach and mother spoke German, were both European and could converse with all of the officials at the World Championships. And they did just that. Scott was groomed since 1960 when his coach paraded him around at the California Squaw Valley Olympic Games. They had the funds and know-how to promote, and they did. He became the fair-haired, curly-headed, young golden boy. They were a PR machine and Fritz Dietrich, his coach, really knew how to work it. He was a real veteran. Coach Don was only 14 years older than me and not experienced at this level, or with Europeans, or in this arena.

Create The Force Behind The Quest!

Now we're off to the '65 World Championships at the Broadmoor World Arena for my first time! In mid-March, trying to fly out of Detroit, a huge snowstorm delayed our trip. What a start! But Colorado was beautiful. We all stayed at the world famous Broadmoor Hotel and Resort which had grounds in excess of 800 acres complete with the equally famous World Arena. This little Italian guy from East Detroit, 8 Mile Road, was really out of his realm! I hadn't been here since the 1961 tragic National Championships, and fatal memories of my skating buddies entered my mind. Not to mention the fact that there were also 29 competitors, more than I had ever competed against. For French Champ Alain Calmat, this was his tenth World competition. For me, it was only my seventh year of ice skating! He was a legend to me, a three-time medalist, too. Wow, I am in the Big Boys' Club now!

The media expected me to win again. I was wet behind the ears and ended up finishing the very best that any American male did in his first World Championship: Sixth. Allen was second, which was a big blow to me, but it was still a sweet first victory at the Senior World level.

But what could I have expected? I remember the awards dinner and closing ceremonies. The French judge, Mr. Valdez, said to me, "Gary, if only you had done a triple jump I could have put you first." I said, "What? I did my triple toe-loop, my first trick at opening, watch tomorrow on Wide World of Sports and you'll see it." He said, "Oh, no, I am so sorry I missed it. I thought it was a double." Wow, I was crushed! Now I had lost faith in the experience, knowledge and eye of the European judges. Remember, the Cold War was still on full force. The Eastern Block countries like East Germany, Czechoslovakia, Poland, USSR, and Romania all voted together as a block against the West. Japan and Italy wavered, usually.

Sometimes What You Are Looking For, You Cannot See

In 1965 I was at the top of my world: U.S. and North American Champion. Even with a sixth place finish at my first World Championship, I was on a high! Everything but money seemed to come my way!

One beautiful new "green" thing did come my way. I always was a huge car fan, someone who knew every single make and model and engine. Dad made a huge revenue-saving suggestion to the company and through an extensive promotional campaign introducing the new 1965 Mustang he WON a car! It was fantastic with its 280 hp engine, black vinyl top, dark forest green body and real leather bucket seats ... my dream on wheels. I slept in it the first night. I was a king with a new $2,800.00 chariot.

Looking ahead to the 1966 season was both "hot" and "NOT!" Can I do it again? Was it a fluke? Would Scott Allen come back again? After all, he was second in the world and I was sixth. Did I disappoint my country by placing so low at my first World Championships?

I had everything to lose. Being on top was tough, demanding, stressful, fun, and always "on stage." Where do you go from there? Down? Only down? No, I had to show the world, my coach, the club, even myself that I did have "it." But did I? Could I? Would I? This was eating me up very slowly; it was a demanding year with school, exhibitions, shows, and trying to keep in "winning" form. Maybe I should be even better, maybe reinvent myself? But how? Why? Is it even necessary?

To top things off, just about now Mr. Don flew to the east coast very suddenly. When he returned he told me the exclusive Skating Club of Boston offered him the esteemed position as head coach. At that time this was the real home and powerhouse of U.S. skating. He of course said, "I'll be bringing Gary." They politely agreed, but said I would not be representing their Club. Mr. Don answered, "If Gary's heritage is an issue to membership, then put the position where the sun never shines." Well, there went that whole political fan base.

January 1966 ... U.S. Nationals. Funny things happen in California, and they did once again.

Being Number One Can Be Lonely

This is Berkeley, California, in 1966: Love and hippie time, long hair and flower children. The location was Iceland Arena, packed with skating fans awaiting the battle of the year: Visconti versus Allen. The schedule was running two hours late and the crowd was hungry for a battle with fans of both top challengers in the audience.

I was on the five-minute warm-up, the last group of five top male competitors. It was the most dreaded part of any competition for me, with the judges watching and the fans cheering every major move of their favorite skater. I had drawn second to last to perform; Scott Allen achieved the coveted spot of last.

I remember my name announced and gliding out slowly to my starting position. It was calm now and there was dead silence. I looked up at the clock on the scoreboard and it was 12 midnight. I thought, I wish it was 12:05, and I would be finished. What a way to think! Well, that's just how my performance went. I did not complete three of my major tricks, and each time I missed I had more "juice," more "pizzazz," more smiles, and more performance ... more audience connection. Funny how we try to wing it and cover up under pressure. It was a great performance, but one with too many errors. Scott won. Guess I gave it to him. It was a super life lesson for me and just what I needed! Second place felt like 20th place.

Come Back From Your Setback

So, anyway, I was second place. Yes, Scott had his revenge. He nipped right by me and won the Championship back, and I learned my lesson. Don't doubt yourself! Don't try to figure out the future because you will miss out on today. Just always do your very best — not perfect — but your best. Let the chips fall every day and stay happy and in a good mental place. Push but be patient. As I have heard it said, "It takes a long time for good things to happen, and quickly for bad!" Losing seemed so quick, so bad, and so final. Could I come back?

To Keep The "Edge," You Must Stay Sharp

Now I had to get revenge — to win back my clout and my prestige. Three weeks later in Davos, Switzerland, at the World Championships in the outdoor ice stadium I would beat Scott and captured my first World medal. As I remember it, my start order for the long program was thirteenth (Carol Heiss's favorite number) out of something like 28 competitors.

I do remember stepping off the ice (no security, no kiss and cry area) right into the arms of my new biggest fan, Monica Torriani. Her mom ran the music room and her father was a famous Swiss Olympian, ice hockey player and skier. Monica herself was an elite skater. Well, flowers came my way at the hockey rail, and then a fan threw something for me to catch. I missed and it went on the ice as the next competitor went out. It was a little Swiss Troll, with "Einstein" crazy green hair. Even Dick Button was surprised. I guess this was the first toy tossed in fan appreciation, ever! He proudly sits on my desk today.

When my marks went up just after my performance, they were all 5.8s and 5.9s. I could not imagine who could or would do much better. It didn't seem fair to the 15 other skaters, but I was proud and completely happy. My standing in preliminaries was fourth so a medal seemed in sight. I could hold my head up high now! Even though I was not the U.S. Champion, I was now on the podium at worlds! And the Olympics were only 23 months away! It was all within my reach. What can I expect now? Can I hold on, accepting the challenge?

After the medal ceremony at the open-air arena, and photo opportunities and interviews on the ice, we had a full afternoon ahead. Our event started at 10 a.m. for live ABC television coverage in the United States.

Remember this era (1966) was the bitter Cold War era, and a unique experience evolved that day. The East German skater, Ralph Borghard, was a flamboyant and fun guy. His plan was to defect and ask for political asylum in our host country, Switzerland. Four of us conspired to secretly get him on the last train later that day and get him to the consulate office in Geneva. The big challenge was to get Ralph out of the sight of his communist chaperones. We managed to do just that using an athletic celebration as distraction and one of us secretly taking half of his belongings to the train station. Before he was missed and before the closing gala event that night we had him on the train to freedom. A few years later, Oleg and Ludmila Protopopov made the same decision, defecting from Moscow, and they settled in Switzerland for over 25 years. They now reside in the United States.

That year I went on a six-week exhibition tour of world champions all over Europe. Mr. Don went along as a team chaperone, coach and coordinator. At the Queen's Ice Palace near Hyde Park in London, England, Peggy Fleming and I and several other European champions skated for Queen Elizabeth. A command performance, it was captured on the BBC television network. Royalty is so impressive and demanding of respect. The bows before and after our performances were rehearsed for one hour prior to the show. This was quite a rattling experience. I was only 21 years old — neat and cool, I thought. Harry Lauder, manager of the Queen's Ice Palace, gave us the etiquette do's and don'ts. Of course, we all made fun of everything.

Now onto East Germany.

"You go first," I said.

"No, you go," she said. It was freezing and snowing and the East German guards looked really stern. I was 21 and she was about 15. The Berlin wall stood ominous and solid, cold cement and sharp barbed wire. Janet Lynn pushed me through that scary 100-foot walkway first. My blood ran cold and that walk seemed like miles. I was shaking for sure.

I thought, "Okay, if I get shot she won't cross over. Lucky her." It was the height of the Cold War. East Germany. So scary, and we were so inexperienced.

Not All See The Road Ahead The Same

Now in Karl Marxstadt, East Germany, we skated to a full outside arena despite the rain and the 5,000 black umbrellas filling the bleachers. The show must go on! I skated to my "Irma la Douce" program and did three encores to "Zorba the Greek." Of course we were dripping wet the whole time, but it was a great experience and we were so warmly greeted by the East Germans. It was an honor to perform for them, and they were starving for excitement and heroes.

Now in Moscow, this was our 14th tour exhibition, skating at the National Stadium of Moscow. We performed for Premiere Kosygin and the first astronaut in space, Yuri Gagarin. This was so thrilling!

Being American and also U.S. Champion and World medalist, I felt a responsibility to bring down the house. Some 18,000 people were in the stadium. When I skated to "Zorba the Greek," a very ethnic, fun, foot-stomping and clapping program, it really went over well. Three encores and two standing ovations!

Walking through the city our second day with Vlad as my guard and guide, I couldn't help but notice several street musicians with a unique string instrument. I was captivated by it. Like a banjo, three strings, but made with precision like a beautiful violin. I really wanted one. Vlad took note and the next day we were in a shop to purchase one. He had secured one at a price that my three-day spending money could afford: $16.00. In fact, I think he bought it for me. It hangs on my wall still. I never did learn how to play it. The next month the National Skating Magazine featured me on the cover — a fantastic artist conception of me flying through Red Square and Saint Basil's Cathedral, and of course mentioning my prized musical possession.

At the formal reception after the show I received a beautiful sterling silverware set, a 12-place setting which I still use today. I am sure it went way beyond our usual gifts of under $25.00. Later I was told Mr. Don complained to the Soviets that "Mr. Visconti should receive a special honored gift for his tremendous success on tour in your country." Thus the silverware. He never told me about his demand.

The next day we flew on "Aeroflot" to Kiev in southern Georgia. I remember during the flight there was some disturbance going on with the stewardess and cabin attendants, and the conversation was weird! Then, a uniformed man came out of the cockpit, pulled back the carpet on the walkway between our seats, opened a trap door, and went down under the belly of the airplane. He was gone for some 10 minutes, came back up, and all we could figure out was that the landing gear was stuck and the wheels could not go down for the landing. Guess he had to do it manually. After a few circles of the airport, we landed. Mrs. Fleming was a shaking mess, and I was sitting next to her.

It was here in Kiev that American jeans were a hot commodity. I was offered $200.00, and this was in the 1960s. I gave away our U.S. pins, gum, signed photos ... but I did keep my jeans. I didn't need that international trouble, or to be jean-less.

I remember on the night after our last show in Kiev, one of the European champions asked me to go out with him after hours. Dumb me, I said sure! So we slipped out of the hotel with no guards with us, skipped past the female guards at each elevator, down the back stairs and into the cold, wet, slushy snow. We walked about 10 minutes and met two guys in a very dark and deserted street or alleyway, freezing. Some envelope or money was exchanged, and a small package was then presented to my friend, about 14 inches square. Later at the hotel he came to my room and showed what was in the package: Two old church icons. He was going to resell them in the West. I almost died. How was he going to smuggle them out of Russia! This wasn't legal, was it? Then I remembered, we are sports celebrities. Whenever we went through customs, in any country, they never even looked in our luggage. They just flagged us through. We traveled as an elite sports team. Wow, I was learning about a different life and it was crazy, weird, and uncomfortable, too.

Having Been There Is Not As Great As Where We Are Going Next

Mr. Don and I had to re-strategize and re-create a new training program. I wanted to get back on top of the podium again. Coach Don was making a major move from Detroit, Michigan, to East Lansing, Michigan — some 100 miles away from my parents — and closing his two ice skating studio rinks. I had to change my university studies from Macomb County Community College, near Detroit, to classes at Michigan State University, East Lansing, and live with him. It was a new life for me.

Mr. Norris Wold was a fine man of old school honesty, very fair and sharp. He was the university ice arena manager from 1956 to 1969. He helped my family and my skating by sponsoring my total ice time practice. By 1964, Mr. Don was on the coaching staff of Michigan State University. We had some fun people there, off and on the ice! The Pan-Am swim team trained across the street. The French champions, the Canadian champions, the U.S. Champions, even Vera Wang became my friend. She skated very seriously at that time with Mr. Pierre Brunet. He was the world pair champion several times with his wife. Mr. Brunet coached Carol Heiss, 1960 World and Olympic champion, and Donald Jackson, Canadian and World champion, and many others. He helped mentor me so much — about how to handle competitiveness and the ice — and my emotions toward my sport. He really supported us in winning the 1965 U.S. National Title, and also helped with the European scene.

It became a new life for me. I was now living with Mr. Don in his home ... changing cities, changing schools, and reassessing my training habits and goals. I was starting to come into my own in terms of thinking and planning.

In 1967 I was again the number one premier male skater after winning the U.S. title in Omaha, Nebraska, in January of that year. Heading to Omaha for my revenge to win back my U.S. Title, I was a different athlete. Juggling college classes, skating, and a part-time job at the picture framing gallery kept me really busy.

Omaha was really cold but the people were extremely warm. Again, as in 1965, I was first in the school figures. Luck with me, I drew last for the long program. Tim Wood skated third to last, Scott Allen second to last, and I had the coveted spot. Having the advantage of knowing what each competitor completed or did not complete in their program, I could alter my performance if necessary. Mr. Don came to me a minute before I went on the ice and told me to take out my triple jumps because no other skater had completed them. I just had to skate a clean and elegant program with doubles. That took a lot of pressure off me.

Even Dick Button of Wide World of Sports privately interviewed me so his comments would be accurate, but in those days no prescribed moves were required. After the announcing of my name as the last competitor, the house came down. They wanted a champion performance and the air was electric. The first three minutes of my program seemed like only seconds and the energy and enthusiasm from the crowd was like a drug for me. I said to myself, "I am winning, I am winning." We all knew it, and the crowd carried me to victory and to the very top of the podium again.

To Make The Mark You Must Take Aim

The next weekend when Wide World of Sports featured the national championships on television, I will never forget — ever — Dick Button's comment after I won. "Not always the best skater wins, just the one who makes the least mistakes." But isn't that what life is all about? Not making mistakes? Even though he was a big fan of competitor John Misha Petkevich, I guess he didn't understand our game strategy to win.

So now I am in Vienna, Austria, which was hosting the World Championships that year. It is March 1967, really windy and really rainy. Unfortunately for us skaters, it is the 100th anniversary of the Vienna Ice Skating Club and they want to hold all freestyle skating events in the 100-year-old outdoor ice skating stadium. How barbaric is that! To top it off, Emmerich Danzer, World Champion, and Wolfgang Schwarz, also Viennese, and World silver medalist, are on home turf! Their home figure skating club is hosting. How the hell is this little Italian-American boy going to beat them? Sounds impossible!

So back in 1966 in Davos, Switzerland, all three of us were on the podium. And guess what, it is the same picture in 1967 in Vienna, of course. I could have turned inside out and done a quintuplet and never achieved a silver or gold medal that night. I remember during the five-minute warmup prior to our long program, the March wind in Vienna must have been 20 to 25 miles per hour, blowing across the length of the ice. It was so strong that I could barely jump into the wind. I came to Mr. Don standing at the boards during this warm up and said, "How can I open my program with a triple toe loop going against the wind? I will never get off the ground!"

He said, "Gary, I have an idea. Let's turn the opening of your program around so that you jump with the wind." At that moment the referee called us off the warm up. Mr. Don explained to me that I could perform my triple with the wind, and then after that jump turn my program back around the way it was originally set.

I was okay with that.

I remember starting my program and taking off for my triple jump. I felt that the wind carried me 10 feet off the ground. I was airborne, for sure! I thought, "Holy shit!" I was really out of control. It was a huge jump and of course, I fell. I went sliding across the ice thinking, "You really blew it now, Visconti! You'd better do a hell of a job the next four minutes and 15 seconds to make up for this!"

The pressure was now off because I made that mistake, so for the rest of the program I skated with abandon and personality, and had fun. I performed my next triple effortlessly (guess the wind calmed down) and ended up having a fine performance. I went home with a duplicate bronze medal, but won the evening.

The Other Guy Doesn't Have It All

After winning the title in Omaha and then capturing the World bronze medal for the second time, I am now perched to be an Olympic medal winner next season. Wow, the pressure, and I had to figure out how to deal with it.

The Broadmoor Skating Club in Colorado Springs, Colorado, was now the anchoring power and in control of U.S. Figure Skating. They had already secured Carlo Fassi, an internationally famous coach from Italy, and Peggy Fleming last year. Now thrown in my lap was an offer to go train at the Broadmoor World Arena, not with Mr. Don with but Mr. Fassi, and with all expenses paid. I flatly refused. I felt if I can't win the Worlds with my life coach then so be it. Later the positions went to Ron Baker and Tim Wood, and Tim became a World Champion at the Broadmoor in 1969. Lesson learned, but I didn't want to be bought. It was a tough lesson to swallow.

Olympic year is coming and I am all pitched and ready to start training hard eight months before. February 1968, Grenoble, France, the site of the 10th Olympiad for the Winter Games. Just remember, the Vietnam War was raging at this time. The U.S. draft was hot. No guy 18 to 27 could dodge it except for medical reasons, very bad hardship within the family, admitting openly that you were gay — which at the time I considered using as an excuse, but I was exclusively straight at 21 years old — or a full-time college student, and I was enrolled in a 12-credit semester. Well, the college neglected to send the required paperwork on time to the U.S. Military Draft Board office in Michigan, and 121 male students lost their college deferment from military obligation, and I was one of them. On the dreadful day of September 10th I found out about this mistake by receiving a 1-A classification draft notice paper on Monday, and Tuesday in the mail I also received my "Induction into the U.S. Army." Wow, the world just came to an end for me. Twelve years of planning and working daily to get to be number one in America and top three in the world in my sport. Damn!

Mom was so upset that the next day, as she was ironing clothes, put down the iron and went to the phone, got a long-distance operator and said, "I want to be connected to the White House in Washington D.C., and person-to-person to the President, please." What guts she had, and such drive and confidence! People then never would have done that, but Mom was not the norm. She did talk to his personal secretary. I never knew what information was exchanged, but what a Mom!

That evening we had a big meeting with Mr. Don, the family and me. What do we do now?

Being the "special son" of the Detroit Skating Club, to whom I had brought so much pride and national focus for being now twice champion of America, our club president that year was a retired admiral in the U.S. Navy. We called him at his home at 10 p.m. that night. We told him the entire story and he said, "Meet me tomorrow evening at 6 p.m. at the Naval Reserve Center main office and we will fix things." And sure enough I was sworn into the Naval Reserve Program that night as a 2x6er, which meant two years active duty and six years as a reservist, and it was all set to defer my two years of active duty until way after the Olympic Games. That paperwork was post-dated two weeks earlier, before my draft notice from the Army.

The next day I went to my local draft board office downtown to meet Miss Katherine Poole. She was extremely angry and she knew or somehow felt that the whole thing was fixed by the Navy. I heard later that Army and Navy officers fought over the whole thing for four weeks. But SN B584701 was now Gary Visconti, Naval Reservist and figure skater. Special handling of my delicate position was handled by BUPERS Naval Office in Washington and Mr. Ben Lewis. He was great, until the Navy itself made a blunder and sent me orders to report to Great Lakes, Illinois, Naval Boot Camp for eight weeks of training on December 2nd, only 12 weeks before Olympic trials (U.S. Nationals in Philadelphia). Now I was screwed. As the current American champion and World medalist, I could not skate or train for two months. I wanted to die. Word was getting out all across the country and I lost all my life, heart, and confidence in people, America, the government, the Navy. My life was over.

So there I found myself at 6:00 a.m. in downtown Detroit, getting on a bus filled with 52 other young American guys, all of us enlisted. On our way on November 30, 1967, to the Great Lake, Illinois, U.S. Naval Training Center — boot camp for eight full, grinding, bitter cold, hard core, disciplined, lonely, crowded, testosterone-filled, no frills training! All I could think of was my skating competitors practicing six hours a day while I was playing soldier. My outlook for a berth on the Olympic Team in 12 weeks was very cloudy to say the least.

Mr. Joe Searfine to the rescue! Janice, his daughter, skated with Mr. Don and I every summer in East Lansing and we were good friends. They lived in Lake Forest, Illinois, about 45 minutes from the Naval Center and a very affluent area. Joe would pick me up every Sunday while I was on leave and take me skating so that I could at least keep the feel of the ice under my feet for two hours. He was wonderful. They kept my skates at their home and had me for a fun and elegant dinner in their huge home. How bizarre — from barracks to a mansion every week! Well, between toilet cleaning, hiking, push-ups, midnight fire watch, climbing 15-foot fences, crawling in mud, and jumping off 30-meter diving boards (very reluctantly), I became in even better physical shape for a 21-year-old. But, no ice under my feet!

I will always remember the swimming test, even more than going through the 60-foot burning building. I was on the 30-meter board and fourth in line to jump and swim the length of the pool. "Well, I can't swim," I said to the guy behind me, "and I really hate heights." He said "Tough," and then pushed me off the platform.

Thank God I hit the water feet first ... somehow, some way. With the help of my guardian angel I made it to the other end of the pool completely exhausted! I'd rather skate in front of two million people on live TV.

Somehow I made it through all the vigorous, crazy training elements despite my small frame. I didn't break, only mentally. I was beaten and my heart and soul yearned for the ice.

I went to Philly with only eight days of training and lost my U.S. title. I came in a strong second to the ever-threatening Tim Wood. He was all perched and ready to de-throne me with pleasure. It made it worse that he was my fellow club skater in Detroit. Third place went to John Misha Petkevich, a strong athletic and fantastic jumper. Former Olympic Medalist Scott E. Allen did not even make the team, but was named to the World Team because of his previous World placement.

At that championship for the first time in modern history all 13 top male competitors drew out of one pot for the final skating order for the final long free skate program, and I drew number one, probably the worst and most dreaded position ever. Mr. Wood somehow picked last to skate, some 2-1/2 hours after my perfectly clean performance. The crowd was still arriving in their seats while I was skating. Later, the atmosphere was hot and the competition keen. I just watched the title slip away, although I performed my best technical performance ever. That first start position is death. Thankfully, that rule no longer exists.

Now I was chosen for the Olympic team, but what kind of signal was the U.S. sending to the world when they de-throned me and chose a new champion, just 16 days before the Olympics in France? This was a blow which I could not fix. I just kept smiling like a winner, though my heart was dead. The next morning, Sunday, we had a Sports

Illustrated photo shoot for the cover. The Olympic team was just announced the night before, and at the hotel they did two-and-a-half hours of interviews and photos. Peggy Fleming and Tim Wood and the U.S. pair champions were slated, and because I was holding World medals the last two years and had just finished three big interviews for Sports Illustrated, they wanted me in that cover shot, too. Wow, kind of weird, but smile!

The one part I will always remember is the magazine asking me if I thought figure skating should be in the Olympics. My comment to that was, "Do people think that all we do on ice is run around on our crinkly toe picks and skate in brassiere material costumes?" That caused a stir, for sure. Today, skating has evolved to be more like Cirque du Soleil with contorted positions, toe-pick running, real fur and sequins, and lace costumes and brassiere material. Also, the most complex point system every designed by the ice gods.

The 1968 Olympics were here, and my dream event could become a nightmare. The U.S. team had to leave early for France from New York City where we had to get our uniforms and be debriefed. The figure skating team was the last of the 690 athletes to be chosen as a team, and only 16 days before opening ceremonies. Coach Don could not go early (12 days) before the opening of the 14-day Games. He had obligations so he asked Peggy Fleming's coach, Carlo Fassi, an Italian Olympian skater himself, to coach me for 10 days there before he could come to France. Needless to say, Carlo was so busy with Peggy that I received little attention, but he was so good to me there. I was lonely — no parents, no coach, and no longer the champion either, flying solo and low.

Things in the Athletes' Village were strange, too. U.S. figure skaters roomed together. We were not a "team" as we wanted to beat each other on the ice, so there was tension. Also, we practiced very early every day there, and unfortunately for us the U.S. Ice Hockey team lived in the apartment above us and they were on a late schedule and came home noisy and loud. It woke us up constantly, so we used to pound on the ceiling to quiet those guys down. Big help that was. Like they really cared.

To Carve A Niche In Life, Carry A Sharp Tool

Grenoble was a beautiful French village high in the alps, but the weather was not ideal. There was no snow, and the opening ceremonies were to be held tomorrow. What would the officials do? Well, they brought 500 spruce trees and thousands of tons of snow down from the higher mountains and covered the exterior of the temporary stadium. It looked like a Hollywood set on television. The French pulled it off, or at the least world thought so.

One night we were bored. Our team leader, a 55-year-old non-skater named Mr. Carl Graham, was staying on our floor and across the hall. He loved his drinks. One night while he was soundly sleeping we went into his room and filled his sheet with three cans of shaving cream. That was fun, but he never even mentioned it the next day. He was too out of it! During the boring afternoons we dropped water balloon out of our eighth-floor windows onto the entrance below. How childish is that? But we did have good target practice.

There was no snow; it was rainy and 39 degrees. Because the practice schedule was so very bad all the figure skaters, some 96 in all, and hockey teams did not get equal ice time at the new Olympic ice arena. The committee closed the indoor arena to figure skaters and made us practice outside every day for one week in the rain. They were terrible conditions, unheard of by today's standards. We only trained twice on the arena ice with our music played, which was real bizarre. This was the Olympic Games? Oh my God!

I had been there alone for 10 days, and the morning Mr. Don arrived in Grenoble we were walking through the town and into a beautiful little café. Mr. Don stopped in his tracks and turned to me and said, "Don't look now, but sitting at the bar is Audrey Hepburn." I was so impressed with her clean, sweet, beauty. Of course, I went up and introduced myself as a U.S. Olympian. That opened the door for her to ask us all these questions. She loved figure skating and said she would be there for the men's finals and would root for me. I told her I looked forward to her next film and we shook on it. Fun, fun, fun for a 23-year-old guy!

Love Shared Is Harvested In Abundance

So what the hell am I doing here? I have dreamed of this and had a perfect vision of this moment my entire life. I had trained for 13 years, four hours or more each day, for this very moment. I am now standing in front of 16,000 people and they are booing and stamping their feet! There are 100 million people watching all over the world and I am not ready. They just announced my name and my country. Damn! It's the Olympics and the crowd is booing the marks awarded to the previous skater by the judges. Damn you, French people! Now is my chance and they would not quiet down.

I skated over to the judges' box and said to the official referee, "What is going on?"

"Gary, could you calm them down?"

I looked at him with a glare and said, "I have worked for this moment for 13 years – you calm them down!" I skated off to Mr. Don and waited for a minute or so, then took my start position again, signaling the audience to calm down with my hand gestures. In my mind I was thinking, This is not how I envisioned this. I am not ready. I am not even here as a U.S. Champion. I am second and a U.S. Navy man.

Only five weeks ago I had finished the eight-week Navy boot camp at Great Lakes, Illinois, and did not skate at all during that time. Then, I practiced for only 10 short days and lost my U.S. title, barely, to Tim Wood. Now his name was on the trophy. I did not want to be here. This is not how I had envisioned this. I was in sixth place after the preliminaries, whereas last year I was in third place at this point. I was not in a good mental state. This surely was a test ... like I've never been tested before. Okay, just go do it like you have trained a thousand times before. Get into the mode, focus, and feel and control the moment.

If You Hit The Wall, Climb It

Figure skating at the time was divided so that 60 percent of the competition score was figure eights very precisely patterned out on a clean, glassy, new ice surface. You had to be like a precision machine, so perfectly traced one on top of another, usually six tracings. The other 40 percent of your total score was the fun free skate program to music of your choice and with hardly any restrictions. Sometimes a skater could gain a real strong point lead in the figure portion of the competition so that their lackluster freestyle routine — maybe earning them only a third place finish — would still win them the championship because of the total points earned. Many times the fans were disappointed because their favorite freestyle skater did not end up in first place. I was noted for my fun, light, airy freestyle. But funny, I never won a major championship that I was not already first in the figures portion.

Okay, the music is starting for my five minutes and nine seconds of free skate program. Here we go! "Just perform," I thought. The music is taking me, for sure. I am flying. The ice feels so soft and good and fast, and I am loving it! I cannot hear the audience at all anymore. Strange, because I can see them. The music is taking me through and thank God because I am on auto pilot. I have done this routine probably 1,200 times or more in the past two years in preparation for this moment. We did our five-minute warm-up for the group of five skaters almost one hour ago. It takes about eight-and-a-half minutes for each competitor to skate and the scores of 18 judges given aloud and spoken in both English and French. I was worried about that long wait and time off the ice after warm-up but it did not seem to matter. Nothing mattered because I was numb. I felt only speed and the wind and my force. After all, we were in Grenoble training for 12 days and only skated on this Championship ice twice. We had to train outside daily, and it rained for four days! This was not the dream Olympic experience. Kind of like the worst dream! But before I knew it the music had ended. Good, no major mistakes; complete, but not inspiring. Wish I could do it again. No chance.

I don't remember much of the performance itself. Mr. Don was at rink side when I came off and he said, "Well, you made it through." I knew that it was a "flat" performance. No heart, no passion. I did receive a few 5.9s and several 5.8s out of a perfect 6.0, but I only pulled up a little in the finals. My thirst for Olympic gold was gone. Why did I have to come here like this, so unprepared and so self-beaten? The experience seemed empty — not fulfilling at all — like a job you had to do. This was not the blessing from above. Even though I was so very proud to represent the U.S.A. and the U.S. Navy, my personal representation of Gary Visconti to the world stage was unrewarding. Being in the top five was not my goal; an overall medal was.

The closing ceremonies were fantastic, yet sad. We had made so many new friends and would never see some of the wonderful old friends (from communist countries) ever again. The ceremonies were in the closed arena; the crowd was so warm and friendly as the athletes came into the arena as one huge "world team" — no country announcements, just "Your Olympians." No medal announcements, no losers, no countries, only athletes hand-in-hand. It was a really moving moment. I remember the floor was so very crowded and we were packed in like sardines in a can. Behind me were the Russian female pair skaters; Tatyana Zhuk, Olympic Silver Medalist, was in her official track suit. I said to her, "You wanna trade suits?"

She said, "Okay."

"Now?" I asked. "Here, now? Out here?

"Why not?" I told all the athletes next to us to hover around and we changed uniforms right then and there, in the middle of French President Charles de Gaulle's closing speech. I still, to this day, have that super U.S.S.R. track suit, and it still fits. Thank God! I cherish it. My Olympic experience means so much more to me today. Then, it was an expectation of medal success. I now value the life lessons of that 16 days as "Golden. Grenoble. Gratitude."

It was not until I returned home to the States that one of my Olympic moments was realized. Only after watching a re-run of the men's final did I hear Dick Button's commentary on Wide World of Sports. Approaching my triple jump, the pattern was completely "off," and knowing that would not work I re-approached the jump a second time unbeknownst to any observer except Dick Button. He called the trick coming up, then said, "Well, I guess he decided not to do this jump; it's one of the habits of this skater. Oh, yes, now he has. Oh, yes, he has completed the triple. I was wrong." Well, we call this "thinking on your feet" strategy. I knew that first jump would not have been successful and my very long spin combination afterward was cut short to return back to the music cues.

In 2008 I established a new idea for Olympians. I had a special anniversary of my 40th year of the night I did my Olympic performance. I truly feel such a special day in your life should be celebrated at least every four years, with family and friends — a special sport anniversary. Honor yourself, be proud, and share and give back. There was something special the Olympics gave me. Some of my guests included Trifun Zivanovic, Cathy Machado, Charlene Wong, and Olympic Champion Robert Paul. We all shared stories and tales from our experiences, laughed and cried and gave thanks for our incredible experience of a lifetime, one that only a few experience. Without the help and guidance of the very unselfish people centered around us during our lifetime quest, this most elite sport experience would never have happened.

Thank you Mom, Dad, Don, my sisters, and super supporters of my ultimate goals. You live in my being, daily.

Decade 3: Fulfillment

fulfill: to do what is required, such as a promise or a contract ... to succeed in doing, providing, or achieving something true or real.
— Webster's Dictionary

Fulfillment ... a realistic term. How full is your heart? How full is your ego? How full is the future? The present? Your soul? But here "fulfillment" is reaching your first planned goal. The endless self-made quests that can ignite your passion to reach for more, keeping all life essentials in perspective.
— Gary Visconti

Dreams Are For Those Who Strive

The world sees it as amazing — doing what we set out to accomplish. We elite athletes just do what we do, daily, because we love it and it is that driving force within. We set goals, small and large daily, expect our best and take no second best effort. We try always to beat our own standards and records, surpassing our goals. It's just what we do. It is our everyday m.o., expanding ourselves and our sport.

The Light At The End Of The Tunnel Is Lighter And Brighter
Than You Think

Some people think when you accomplish your ultimate goal it's like heaven or winning the lottery or the greatest thing ever. Actually, to me, finally winning the U.S. title and even the World Professional Championships, it was more of a relief and knowing that coach, family and I did it together. All the blood, sweat, tears and money to get that Ph.D., or pass the bar exam, or become an M.D. is worth it. But to me, it was only a steppingstone to the next great adventure, the next great chapter in my life. You do not want to sit on your latest accomplishment too long or it may become sour. Be proud of it, use it, grow from it, remember it, and flourish. Don't forget to plan the next challenge ... it keeps you humble, growing, challenged, young, and eager.

Climbing To The Top Is Difficult, But Staying There Is The Real Test

I was so over-ready to break into professional skating. My parents were so done paying for everything, and Mr. Don was tired of pushing and fighting for me every step of the way for over 13 years. He co-sponsored me, too — lessons, ice time, and all. So after the 1969 World Championships I signed with the Madison Square Garden Corp. They owned "Holiday on Ice," the major ice show company in the world with six shows touring on four continents.

When I turned pro in the summer of 1969, Dwayne Mackie, Terry Tunks, Diana Stall, and Maude DuBois had been Mr. Don's national team. Dwayne avoided the military draft in 1967 as I remember it and went to Canada. This was during Vietnam. He was a buddy, a friend, and a really good skater, and trained with us at

Michigan State University at East Lansing. Dwayne was a very quiet, very small, pale-faced blond boy three years younger than me. He was fast and quick and great at school figures. He was a new senior national competitor while I was the veteran on the ice. He and his Dad and uncle were very close! Mr. Don really helped the boy. His Dad never listened to anyone and always did what he wanted career-wise for Dwayne.

Anyway, in the summer of 1969, he returned from Canada. No one had heard from him and he was now a real lost loner. He was arrested for entering someone's home, as I remember it. He fell asleep there and the owners found him, called the police, and he was put in jail (I think he was under some influence). In jail he was beaten, raped, and died. I was really upset to think another close skating buddy was gone.

At that time I was also dealing with my skating brother Dana Charette. We were close friends since age 14. He was in combat in Vietnam in a U.S. Army helicopter, the gunman in the rear of the chopper killing people on the ground. He wrote to me in every letter how he went numb doing that and felt inhuman. I wrote him very often during those two years to keep him close and sane, and to help me feel like I could then not lose him, too. Dana kept every one of my letters and even made a book of every letter that I sent him, and it is a two-year diary of my life. He presented it to me at my 60th birthday celebration, and I cherish it.

Image on Following Page: One of my many letters to Dana Charette while he served in Vietnam.

Thursday Feb 28-68

Hi there Bones —

Thanks for your letter, was very good content on your part. Yes Grenoble was really some- else; glad you were not there because tomatoes would have flown from your hand. Those crazy french people. Pera the Bronze Medalist is really a laugh. Danzer not even in the running was very shocking to all. Here in Geneva for me things are about the same. Just finished figures today, Wood is in the lead just a little,

WOOD - DANZER - PERA - ALLEN - VISCONTI - NEPALA

Friday we free Skate and I have a lot of work to do again to pull up past Allen & Pera. I am sure Danzer will win & Wood second — — we shall see.

I am not going to go on the tour after the Worlds I just want to come home for a while & rest some. I turned down 5 shows in the states but may go to Scotland March 25th. I sure hope you are fine buddy & that they put you in a good quiet spot in Nam. By the time you get this I will be home in Det. so write me when you can; & let me know how you are earning your money. Take good care of yourself

Cia. Ua

Dana came home in early 1969. He was really dealing with extreme fallout from Vietnam and those issues. No one, including me, could get close to him. Dana became a street actor and protestor of the war, and pulled away from all of us. I had just returned from Europe, telling Dana about the World Professional Championship I had just won at Wembley Stadium in London, England, and the prize money. This was one of the highlights of my competitive career. The field was well represented and once again I drew last to perform, which was a great advantage. All the major ice show presidents and choreographers were there and stakes were high. I performed my favorite routine, "Irma la Douce," and was awarded a perfect 10.0 from two judges. What an honor.

Of course, I was on the road for 10 months with the ice show, with many commitments as a show headliner and I would not make it back to Michigan where Dana was active. As time passed, we became less close, not by choice but because of our lifestyles. I eventually moved out west to California and he was trying to piece his very interrupted life back together. Like so many other war veterans, he was lost, and no one really understood, could help, or wanted to. I felt very unattached from him. Now Dana lives near Los Angeles, married and very happy, and we are close buddies once again. Bones (Dana) and Buns (Gary) are united again.

The Fruit Of Life Can Be Rewarding If You Replant The Seeds

Now that I was a World Professional Champion and had just signed a major contract with the Madison Square Garden Corporation, my amateur days were over. I was a pro. The Holiday on Ice Company based in the United States had six major touring shows in the world on four continents and owned Madison Square Garden Corporation. Because my name was more popular in Europe I was sent to star in the show which toured all of the major cities in Europe. As part of "The Gold Division Company," I am a 23-year-old now and will be living alone; no Mr. Don, no parents and all old friends and family 10,000 miles away. Weird, but exciting. The door was opened ... just step in.

We rehearsed in Nice, France, for six weeks that fall of 1969. I found a moderate hotel; I had arranged while on tour for my salary to be paid in the United States and I received a weekly allotment in cash while in Europe. Otherwise, I really didn't know how to handle the money there. I opened a bank account in Germany to have a base and savings there.

We opened the show in Geneva, Switzerland, in September. I really loved show biz — no judges, skating every day and being paid as one of the highest paid ice artists of the time. Life was great! I was young, single, had money and had five to 10 years in show business ahead of me. This was a major adjustment for me. No Mr. Don or parents to tell me what to do and no one to really answer to. This could have been the big turning point; good and bad, temptation everywhere. Drugs, sex and rock 'n roll were around me, and money, too! The seasoned show people were so good to me. They were a family — and like all families — crazy, cliquey, mixed-up, funny, and drama — lots of drama. And jokes, too, mostly on me, the new "star."

To Fill The Shoes You Have To Jump In

A whole new world was opening for me, and I met so many new people. Ted Shuffle was our famous choreographer. What a character! He knew and worked with Sonja Henie and had produced fabulous work. When I met him I was really taken aback by his frankness and language and style and manner of delivery of information to us. He was a true artist: Real sharp, bright, creative, and he knew exactly how he wanted his show to look. In general, he loved my work. He said I was the most professional amateur skater he had ever met. He was tough on me but he let me be me, and he brought the best out of me.

He also loved drinking and smoking and being flamboyant. He flirted with me and I am sure every other guy in the show. I was always on guard, but was free and happy, too. After all, I could now do whatever I want, whenever. But 15 years of discipline was hard to let go. I had placed all of these restrictions on my conduct and actions. The entire cast of the show and managers also could not figure me out. Was he straight, or gay or asexual? I didn't date anyone but just hung out with several real interesting and cool people. My social skills were good but I really had no experience in dating or relationships — yet. I felt free by not dating anyone or getting involved in that stuff. Drinking was never on my fun list either. I might sound like a square or a prude, but I did not think I was. I always held onto the idea that drugs and sex and rock 'n roll were always there, and that it was your choice to indulge or not.

I practiced daily from 12 to 1 p.m., as long as the ice was available to me. Some of the cast (some 60 skaters) used to make fun and made comments about me taking my skating so seriously — still. After all, I wasn't competing any longer, but for me that was my security ... to be able to perform hard maneuvers during my nightly performances. After all, the show was billing me as a star and paying top money. They expected me to deliver. Each performance I was a little nervous; some of the performers and various acts had been in the show for over 10 years — real gypsies — and to them it was just a job. For me, it was about my career and my status and reputation as a champion. I was always conscious of how people perceived me, what they thought, said and how they reacted. I had been schooled that way through my parents and Mr. Don. Was this good or bad?

Now I wanted to figure out people and my life, my way. Dad always said, "Son, keep everything in perspective." Mom always said, "Look before you leap." Between the two of them I've felt cautious about life, and I had just lived through the 1960s in America (flower children, etc.). Loosen up, Gary! Try to see life through your new eyes now! You're on your own, so grow up, smell the roses, and live life.

Life Is Full Of Twists And Turns — Hang On!

Teddy did two wonderful and different numbers for me. One was a 32-minute production number; I went in and out six times in that production. People today still remember his genius in that. It was a counterpoint production — "Hair" and "Swan Lake" music and that look; classical versus hippie. Of course I was the leader of the classical, blue tights and adorned with a crystal 6-1/2-pound mirrored vest with a white puffy blouse shirt (very ballet).

I do remember one dreaded thing on my mind prior to turning professional. I always said with these bow legs of mine, they'd better not put me in tights in the professional ice show some day! The joke was on me. Yes, that is just what happened. I have always been conscious of my bow legs. If they were straight this 5' 3" guy would be 5' 9". Ha ha! With tights and sports, you have to worry about everything being in the right place and not moving around and causing people to notice. There were always some comments. At least they were flattering!

Beautiful Feelings Are Not Hard To Find; Look Within, Cherish

I really felt like I could fit in just fine. Well, here I was, the big champion ... a star. Not a smoker, not a drinker, not a night owl clubbing type of guy. I was totally boring as far as the adult social life. What did I know of that "show life?" I was an athlete. Anna Galmarini, Italian Champion and Heinz Kroll, her then husband, took me under their wing and always made me feel welcomed. Heinz helped keep my skating sharp with a little coaching each week and Anna, an ice show veteran, showed me the do's and don'ts of show life. Don McPherson also gave me pointers. My competitive friend Hana Maskova, the Czech Champion and third at Worlds, went pro like me just out of amateur competitive life. She was the female star skater in the company and she and I were close friends. She was like a sister to me.

Hana and I worked throughout the 32-minute production with heavy responsibilities. I remember our closing night in Paris after a grueling six-week run there. Hana wanted to drive to the next city in her own car which she had on the tour. It was really raining — April, I think — and I begged her not to leave that Sunday night. "Leave in the morning so you'll be fresh and maybe the storm will be over." Well, she left because her boyfriend was already there waiting for her. I never saw her again. The third death in my skating life. I really missed her, lots and lots. My counterpart from my competitive days was gone. What a blow! I should have made her go out and eat with us after closing night like we always did. I could not even attend the funeral or say goodbye, because the show must go on! Shit. My friend had an understudy to fill the void, but what a huge loss, again. Another life-death lesson.

I again had to relive the loss of all my skating buddies and especially Dougie, seven years ago. Will this ever go away? I must learn how to live with loss through death. It is a part of life that I am learning even now.

Always Be Ready For Your Final Departure

Posing with some of my awards.

The 1965 North American Championships.

Holiday on Ice

WORLD'S LARGEST PRODUCER OF ICE SHOWS
Address reply to:

1801 Nicollet Ave.
Minneapolis, Minn.   55403

October 27, 1969

Mr. & Mrs. Visconti
8401 - 18 Mile Rd.-Apt. 252-C
Sterling Heights, Mich. 48078

Dear Mr. & Mrs. Visconti:

    I have just returned from Europe where I saw the
new show in Berne. I want to thank you for your wire of
good wishes, and I want to tell you that we are all proud
of Gary Visconti.

    Gary is the most professional amateur that I have
ever seen, and in his first appearance already has the
knack of showmanship and professional timing that usually
does not come to other amateurs until two or three years
after they have joined, if ever.

    I do want to take this opportunity to tell you that
you should be proud of your boy. He is really a fine
gentleman. Everybody in the show loves him, and we are
happy to have him with Holiday on Ice. He has conducted
himself like a real pro and is always willing to try.
What is more, he is skating beautifully--I would say, almost
as good as Donald McPherson, who has had many years of
experience as a pro. We hope that Gary stays as nice as
he is, and that he enjoys his professional career. Remember
if there is anything we can do for Gary, please feel free
to call on us.

    Kindest regards.

Yours sincerely,

HOLIDAY ON ICE, INC.

Morris Chalfen, President

MC:jah

CC: Don Stewart

CABLE ADDRESS
"HOLICE" (All Offices)

A nice letter from the head of *Holiday on Ice*.

Me, Peggy Fleming, Vlad and our interpreter.

Meeting Ed Sullivan!

Winning the World Professional Championship in 1969.

My Olympic publicity photo.

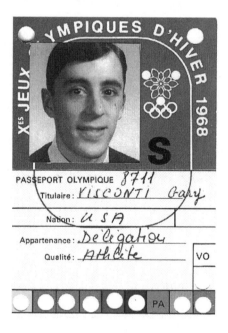

My Olympic credentials.

Sports Illustrated photo shoot.

Regaining the U.S. Title in 1967.

Next we had to open in Lausanne, Switzerland, our first show without Hana. I remember it was a Saturday and we had a three-show day: 4 p.m., 8 p.m. and midnight. It is 11:45 p.m. and we are given show corrections (changes for each performance). The show director said, "I know it's been a long day and difficult without Hana. I want a great show tonight even though it is a midnight show, because Charlie Chaplin is sitting front row center." I felt my heart deflate out of my body. I went numb, thinking Oh my God! My life hero! Actor, director, producer, choreographer and legend Charlie Chaplin is here and I have to perform for him live! Now I must put myself in the performer frame of mind and produce a great, fresh experience.

I immediately turned into performance mode. My solo was an 11-minute number, working with, playing with, and tantalizing six lovely girls. I am a real comedic Don Juan, playing one against the other and ending up losing them all ... just like life. After the show I had the honor of meeting Charlie Chaplin. I was more nervous than when I met the queen a couple of years earlier. I said to him, "You have really inspired me by your life's work," and he said, "Thank you, I truly enjoyed your performance tonight." I was all sweaty and weird and could not speak. He was very gracious and humble. He passed away about five years later.

Speak Your Dreams, They Will Listen

I feel our destiny is set, mapped out for each of us. Our future goal is there for us. We don't know what it is, but the destiny is pre-set. The wonderful creative choice we have is how we get to that goal.

Which path will we take? The long, hard course? Will we use people and things in a bad way to reach our pre-set goal? Will we take people along the way and help? Will we cheat to get there? Will we leave destruction along our path? Will that path we have chosen leave scars on us? Or, can we take the fair, kind, gentle route? Character will show, character will rebuild, and character could be destroyed as we see that goal close, within our grasp! It's all your choice as to how you get there. That's the test, the lesson.

Let Go Of Perfect

I chose a very demanding, exact, precise, yet very imprecisely judged (ranking based on opinion) sport — amateur men's figure skating. At 11-3/4 years of age, when I started taking serious lessons, I had no idea of how demanding and precise the standard was for my future in the sport. At that time the very intricate patterns of the 69 different school figures commonly took six to seven years to learn, practice, then pass the very rigid eight tests. Coach Don really pushed me through those eight tests, as well as three freestyle tests in just 4-1/2 years, and that was quite a feat! And not without criticism. The amount of hours we put in each and every week was roughly equivalent to what most skaters at that time would put in every month of their practice. There is a great book called The Outliers by Malcolm Gladwell which did a long and thorough study of the great achievers — people who excel at music, art, sports. The book concludes one needs 10,000 hours of complete dedicated study before they can bloom. I have estimated that I spent about 9,600 hours when I won my first U.S. National Senior Championship. Guess that book is for real!

This concept of executing those 69 figure eights on perfectly clean, glassy ice and to skate on one foot and on one edge (each skate has two edges, an outside and an inside edge), creating perfectly symmetrical circles with over 40 different turns all lined up as if perfectly traced on the ice, as in the printed rule and standards book ... all this could, if you let it, drive you nuts. It is crazy to try to be perfect! Talk about frustrating. It would be like playing basketball, but the object would be to make a basket every single time you shot while on one leg, using one hand, and with one eye shut ... while balancing on another basketball! Besides the figures, there is the five-minute free skate program to music, with choreography and spins and double and triple jumps all landed on one foot, eloquently choreographed and looking effortless. Effortless my butt! You are working like hell to make it look effortless, trained in the same routine to music about 2,500 times to perform the program just once. Every mistake is calibrated by a complicated microscopic point system. That point system alone could drive you nuts. So with all this "perfection" hanging over one's head every hour of every practice of every day, is it no wonder that one could be a perfectionist? Something to haunt you the rest of your life! I'm still working on overcoming this today.

One day during practice when I was about 19 years old, I realized after many mistakes that I would never be perfect, and I came to terms with that. I let go of perfection, opened my door, and relaxed and really became good. Good enough to become the U.S. Champion for the first time. I realized that I did not have to be perfect, only the best of the group! After all, I was not competing against God! I then looked at my opposition and realized that they were not perfect either. They were just other guys trying to do their best, too, with even more problems and concerns and insufficiencies than me. They were probably more afraid of me than I was of them! Since then I am never afraid to try any new venture, concept, or idea, knowing it may not work out as planned but always trying wholeheartedly to make it work. I always keep in mind that I can make mistakes — after all, I am NOT perfect! Thank the universe.

Have I The Right To Be Successful?

"Gary," I tell myself, "just keep those mistakes small ones." But know one very special lesson: You learn through your mistakes. I really never learned much when I won a championship, but the extremely valuable lessons I learned when I lost stayed with me my entire life. Those lessons have been my base — my foundation — for life. To build on that foundation and collect great builders and workmen (and women!) along the way, on my team, while learning about life and what it offers us.

Decade 4: Loving

love: a: a feeling of strong or constant affection for a person b:
attraction that includes sexual desire c: the strong affection felt by
people who have a romantic relationship d: a person you love in a
romantic way.
— Webster's Dictionary

Love ... a four-letter word with as many definitions as stars in the
heavens. A small word with bountiful capabilities; as huge as the
galaxy. We can love many different ways — things, people, and
cherished visions. Love, we can never define its boundaries. It is
endless, and we are love.
— Gary Visconti

If Love Is So Wonderful, Why Does It Hurt?

It's funny ... when love hits there never seems to be a warning.
I was about 26 and not looking for romance, let alone a significant
other or a wife. I had a very serious girlfriend, Wendy Jones, during my
21st to 25th years, and she was truly a wonderful and sweet girl. We
met on ice. She was a national competitor and eventually came to train
with my coach, Mr. Don, in East Lansing. The crippling of our

relationship was when we both signed professional contracts after winning the World Professional Championships in London, England. She was sent to Asia and I went to Europe, half a world apart. We tried but the distance and our pro commitments were too much. When I came back to the States in late summer of 1970 to replace Ronnie Robertson as a star in the Holiday on Ice tour, that's when I met Juanita.

Love Is A Gift You Give Yourself

I was in my mid-twenties but felt 17; I was not worldly at all about life, girls, sex, and money, and was just learning about being alone. I was on the road in strange cities and countries with strange, jaded show biz people. I always tried to fit in but they were so much more experienced in life. Too much temptation of all kinds ... trouble around every corner. An immature little Italian guy from East Detroit was out in the fast world alone and free. I was tested and kept to myself a lot. I felt great skating in front of 15,000 people, or for royalty or Olympic judges, but to talk one-on-one to a beautiful girl? That was scary. What if I really like her? Then there were the guys who always wanted my attention too and they let me know it. I was a little out of my realm so I just stayed solo for one year, watching and learning. They, the show people, thought I was weird. Not with girls or boys, only married to my skates. That was my "safe zone," where I felt most comfortable.

After a very successful tour all over Europe, Holiday on Ice brought me back to America to star in our very successful European Extravaganza.

That's when I met Juanita Percelly! She was the same age but had been in show biz for 23 years already, born into a circus family in Europe. The Percellys were very famous and very different from any disciplined, nurtured, organized life as mine really was. One town, one family, one great cause in life, solid parents all the way. Juanita was a wonderfully beautiful, strong, fun, alive, talented, shy, bold woman who knew what she wanted. From German and Spanish families, she was never formally educated but extremely "street smart" and "life smart," and spoke five languages. I was very attracted to her in all aspects, and everything about her was exhilarating. My co-star Anna Galmarnie, a veteran performer, was also transferred with me to the national company in the States. She was strong-minded and cocky, but real good. She and Juanita clashed at first but then immediately became close friends. I was happy about their friendship.

The company show manager was ex-performer Tommy Collins, and he made me feel very welcomed but I was cautious. Previously, the show star was Ronnie Robertson, probably one of the ice world's most naturally talented athletes of all time. He was a genius ice skater who had won the World Freestyle event for several years but was never crowned overall champion. Most experts say it was because of his "flamboyant lifestyle" in a very conservative and subjectively judged sport. He was very openly gay in the 1950s, which was not accepted at all by the ice skating community. Tom Collins had constant demands and situations with this performer and was cautious when I replaced him. I had my work cut out to gain his confidence. It took time as our friendship grew, and his brother was married to Juanita's sister.

Juanita was having big marital problems with her skating partner and husband of 2-1/2 years, Tommy Allen. She and I used to talk, a lot, everywhere. She would tell me her concerns and her insecurities, and everything about her 1-1/2-year-old daughter, Tasha. I would listen and give a little advice, but mostly just listen. She loved that and for months we bonded. Then she loved me. She always said, "How can someone like you always be happy?" It was just me. There for her, listening and caring.

Big trouble now — Visconti breaks up the ice love couple, Tommy and Juanita. I was the bad guy, or so the rumor spread everywhere, worldwide.

Well, not so. One person does not break up a relationship of two people. It was already bad, stressed, and they were living separately. Everyone thought we were sleeping together but we did not start doing that until much later than everyone else thought. She was my first real love. We would always talk and hang out backstage, nothing to hide. We were only friends then but as the months went on everyone accused us of having an affair. That came much later. She would be the first woman I slept with, and for me it was a whole new maturity. We then had to hide and sneak and cover up, at least so we thought.

The tension between her and her husband became so strained that the ice show management became very concerned. All the performers in the show started taking sides. Tommy eventually left the tour and Juanita's contract was terminated (even though she had signed a solo contract, not as a member of a pair). Penny Singleton, the union representative, did not support Juanita on the individuality of those contracts. So Juanita traveled on tour with me, not working, through Mexico City.

Don't Be Afraid Of A Little Dirt In Life

I remember one special time on tour while Juanita was traveling with me trying to evaluate her life now. We had just bought a basset hound; he was named Snoopy, so funny. Juanita had just taken Tasha back to their home in New Mexico where Tommy and the grandparents could have some time with her. Juanita returned to the show tour in Florida. Anna Galmarini's husband-to-be and key stage hand Jules Mayer and I rented a very nice houseboat and we all lived on it for three weeks and piloted it through the inter-coastal waterways around southern Florida, instead of living in hotels, and we had great fun. Snoopy learned how to swim and had a new dog-life experience, too.

I was able to use some my Navy skills, too. After all, while traveling on tour it was still mandatory for me to attend Naval Reserve and check in bimonthly at a center along the ice show tour. How weird was that!

After her husband left the ice show in the middle of the tour he went back to their beautiful home in New Mexico. They divorced, and I did not go back to Europe in the show the next season. Our U.S.A. tour was bought out by Ice Follies and that was the end for us. Anyone of star-performer level was not rehired. I guess all things happen for a reason.

After a bad, expensive child custody lawsuit with Tommy, we got married and we won custody of our Tasha and could start our married family life and put all this mess behind us.

Obstacles Are Abstract

Out family photo taken in Los Angeles in 1976.

Me and Juanita!

My family was not happy at all about a divorced woman with a two-year-old kid. How bad is Gary? Guess the pillar fell. Dad was very cold about the whole thing. Mom was so cool but more accepting. Juanita was a lot to handle and I was growing overnight into a husband and a dad in no time. Yes! I was also feeling the strain of my family. Mr. Don was very verbal to me not to do this. The whole world was against us! My stability was shaken and our relationship was challenged constantly by the world around us.

Word spread throughout the ice skating world like wildfire, both in pro and amateur circles. Did you hear about Visconti breaking up a marriage? Well, Juanita and I remained strong and never cried on anyone's shoulder, and I jumped into controversy with both feet.

Laugh And Love This Life Away Because It Will Laugh At You

Leaving the ice show life and the prestige, travel, freedom, and good money was hard. The universe did tell me to stop because our U.S. company was sold and Holiday on Ice President Morris Chaffen wanted me to return to Europe. After all I was only two seasons in his company and he was extremely proud of my work, and I think of me, too. Well, Juanita and I were now very serious about trying to finish her divorce and her marriage of 2-1/2 years with her skating partner Tommy Allen. There was that name again. Allen. Like Scott Allen, and competing for a whole new game — a lady, a wife, and a life partner. Challenged again, and struggling.

I went to my hometown of Detroit to feel comfortable and was immediately offered the Senior Head Coach position at the Detroit Skating Club. I had never taught for any extended period of time and now had to be a head coach and director. It was a big responsibility and a new proving ground both professionally and personally. I was getting used to pressure now for us three.

My father was very Italian and very old school Catholic. Juanita and I were handling her divorce and were living together, but Dad was very opposed to that. He pulled no bones about it either! He told us he would never come to visit us until we were married, and that took almost one year. Detroit was good to me. We were married on April 3, 1971, and started our life together.

A long, dirty, and expensive custody battle broke out but Juanita won and Tasha became ours. I truly respected her father and let her visit him whenever he wished. I also cherished her as my daughter and my little shining star. I wanted to show she was mine — to nurture and love and cherish — and be her dad.

By the summer of 1972 Mr. Don was already established in coaching in Phoenix, Arizona, and begged me to come and team coach there with him. Juanita and I felt like getting away from Detroit was a good idea; we could really bond as a new family. After all I was now a husband, a dad, and a coach all at once, and only 28 years old! I felt a lot of responsibility now and had to really work for the money, not just perform 28 minutes a night for a huge paycheck like in the ice show. Juanita walked away from her marriage and took nothing and wanted nothing from it except her precious daughter Tasha. Tasha was her life. I truly respected her for that and she was a stay-at-home mom and devoted to us at such an early stage, and always did the best she could.

It was tough being thrown into parenting all at once. Thank God and the universe that I had the greatest role models. Mom and Dad were loving but tough about moral character and tradition. We were an

Italian family and Dad was really stuck in the old world mentality while Mom tried to be "modern." This was a slight yet constant struggle between them. I can see that now in later life and looking back.

Tasha was a handful — she was weaned in the ice show from birth to 2-1/2 years old, traveling all the time with Mom and Dad and in a different hotel every week, a different bed, and with a different babysitter always. Not a very stable start. She seemed extremely uncomfortable and insecure, and dealing with that was extremely hard for Juanita, who didn't have skills for that role but did her very loving best, always. The strained marriage with her skating partner Tommy certainly did not help, which of course led to a divorce after only 37 months of marriage.

How Much Love Can I Give?

Moving to Phoenix seemed to be the answer for us to get a fresh start. Mom drove out with us and on that three-day trip the three of us bonded. Juanita truly adopted Mom as her mom. She needed nurturing and Mom loved her and understood her, which was a true blessing. We bought a four-bedroom, three-bath house on two acres with a pool and horse privileges on our land in Scottsdale, Arizona. We were really set, and bonding. Our second daughter Michele came in August of 1973, a little bundle. Tasha was now five and loved playing mother to her baby sister. All seemed to be fusing together and growing.

After 3-1/2 years there I wanted to be a big coach — Worlds, etc. — so we moved to California. Phoenix was too young and small in the skating world in the early 1970s. Phoenix only had one ice rink and if I could fulfill my dream of being a good national and world coach it was not going to happen in Arizona.

Although I did develop and attract several top skaters to the desert, it was slow. Perry Jewell lived with us and became a medalist at the National Junior level and then decided to follow me to my next big challenge.

Los Angeles, here I come!

Does Anyone Really Know How To Love?

In Detroit and then Phoenix and now Los Angeles, I was jumping into being a husband and immediate father. I went from being single and making great money and loving stardom to working hard daily and living in one place trying to establish a client base of competitive figure skaters. Also, I was learning how to deal with all of their crazy, insecure problems and dealing with the stressed out parents spending money on their kids' careers and not knowing if it was wasted or not! I grew up real fast from 29 to 32 years old. Solving other people's problems with elite sports and the very complicated dynamics between parents and kids was challenging but extremely helpful in my new family relationship and dealing with my two little girls – a newborn and a 5-year-old. My beautiful and talented wife, Juanita, was never really nurtured by her family. She had so many childhood obstacles to overcome. Her father was captured and put in a Russian prison camp during the war, from 1943 to 1947. He came home when she was four and went right back into the circus performing life and of course took the family with him, his meal ticket.

They were all tumbling and high wire acrobats in the Althoff Circus, which is still in Europe today. Juanita was forced to perform daily; her father was a tough taskmaster and spending over three years in a prison camp made him worse. Dealing with abuse and having to perform as a child left her with many scars and issues. I thought I could and would change all that and teach her a beautiful, peaceful, and loving secure new life now. I was killing myself to do that and never gave up on that effort.

When she was 11 the ice show hired their act; the father left the family and deserted when Juanita was 12. By age 16 her mother died and the three children, ages 16, 19, and 21, were in the U.S. working still in the only thing they knew, professional ice shows. Juanita fended for herself and by the time she was 22 had landed her skating partner Tommy Allen, secured herself a spot in professional skating history, became one of the top acts in show business, was nominated for a Toni Award for a live performance, had seven Ed Sullivan Show television appearances and a Cinerama movie part. She made her mark even though her father (only in her life for seven years) said that the family would be nothing without him. She had a lot to deal with, but Gary to the rescue ... so I thought.

Life Is Full Of Twists And Turns ... Hang On!

Being a dad with two daughters was challenging. The toilet seats were always down in our house. With a wife and two daughters (even our two dogs were female), I was forced to pee sitting down, thus feeling a small loss of manhood on a daily basis; it was just easier. I would usually forget to put the seat down and my little ladies would fall in. I was always in trouble at home about that, constantly.

Love can move mountains and level them also. Juanita and I were extremely challenged by a world that judged us and never knew all the facts and circumstances surrounding our decision to stick it out and make it work, get custody of our daughter Tasha and be married. Yes, love can make or break you. In my case it gave me strength, and I loved it. It's something I can always cherish. I was truly blessed.

Decade 5: Sharing

sharing: 1: to divide and distribute in shares: apportion — usually used with out <shared out the land among his heirs> 2a: to partake of, use, experience, occupy, or enjoy with others 2b: to have in common <they share a passion for opera> 3: to grant or give a share in — often used with with <shared the last of her water with us> 4: to tell (as thoughts, feelings, or experiences) to others.
— Webster's Dictionary

Sharing ... A lesson mandatory for marriage and parenting. Nothing is yours — only your heart — and everyone is playing tug of war with it. Give, give, give, provide, nurture and guide the family. No real previous experience has made you ready. Your instinct, love, and intuition will guide you. Good luck!
— Gary Visconti

Love Shared Is Harvested In Abundance

One of the most difficult concepts for our modern age to respect is sharing. So many people feel entitled to selfishly "owning" it all. Just value the building blocks of marriage and parenting. You learn real fast to sacrifice your wants for your young family. This builds strong bonds between all members of the family to share everything, even hardships. All of a sudden before you know it you can't get what you want because it must go to the family. No more "self." It's now us, and them first.

You figured, "Hey, I do know what it's about ... the family. After all, I came from a family." Well guess what ... you are now responsible for the wellbeing and future and security and growth of your family. A whole new perspective and responsibility. How can I learn all this now? I had the advantage of great role models in my own parents. Juanita, on the other hand, had none. This is a challenge, and the "you" is really "we."

Making Waves Can Be Good If The Current Moves In The Right Direction

Los Angeles, and a new home! I was sought out by the Ice Capades Ice Chalet Rink Division. At that time the big ice show company had some 16 rinks in America and was growing. The company wanted me to become involved, so I became Figure Skating Director and Head Coach of the Santa Monica Ice Capades Chalet, where renowned coach John Nicks was coaching and controlling all 16 Chalet rinks and their coaches and skating staff. From 1974 to 1980 was a period of great learning and coaching advancement for my career.

Mr. John Nicks was a top upcoming world coach. He was a World Pairs Champion in the early 1950s and was also my mentor. He taught me so many political and social aspects of high-level coaching and I did help him at that time with technique, especially on single skating and jumping. He was not only a terrific director but became a very good friend as well. I credit him for giving me my jump start into international coaching. By 1975 I was at Worlds again, not on the ice but helping as a coach. It was an honor in 1979 to stand next to Mr. Nicks during the performance at Worlds in Canada when Tai Babilonia and Randy Gardner won the World Championship Pair Title. The die was set and I was able to move on to a record of 29 U.S. Nationals, five Olympics, and 19 Worlds as coach or team leader for various countries including Mexico, India, Australia, Croatia, Korea, Canada, and the United States. What an international record!

Mr. Nicks took me under his wing and I watched and learned his special people skills and the politics of this sport. He in turn picked my brain on technique and skill ideas for jumping and spinning. I felt so comfortable with him, and the 1975 Worlds in Colorado Springs were only six years after my last World performance there.

Coaching seemed like a whole new experience and a whole new level, and what an awakening! I had to learn to give, share, and communicate my knowledge. Our Ice Chalet in Santa Monica was the training mecca of the western United States. On any given day we had on the ice two U.S. National Novice, two Junior, and about four Senior elite competitors; three different countries of National Champions and three World competitors.

I had my own skaters — one National Senior male competitor, Junior pair team medalists and one National Novice skater out of my group of 12 sectional and regional competitors. That was my core team. Perry was now training and qualifying for the Senior Nationals and making an outstanding showing, even though his eyes were set on a featured role as a professional in our Ice Capades show, which he clinched later. I was helping train Tai and Randy and coached their individual moves, jumps, and spins. Mr. Nicks was the pair coach and head coach. I also trained the female Korean Champion and Australian male and female champions, and the 1976 Olympics were around the corner.

Soak Up The Facts And Spread Them Around

In February 1976 Dorothy Hamill became Olympic Champion. The sweetheart of the ice, the "wedge" haircut, sunglasses, her brand and all. Turning pro that March of 1976, she signed a very lucrative contract with a huge appearance fee for that time. Being with the Ice Capades Chalet's and in the Los Angeles headquarters for the Capades office, I became close with the company and its president, Mr. Eby. And he, of course, knew the extensive show performance background of my wife Juanita. They offered her a position to travel in the show with Dorothy and be a companion for her (then 19 years old) and help her adjust to professional life and keep her organized. They became very close friends, with all the good and bad and changing things that go with that. We now had our two daughters — Tasha, 9, and Michele, 4 — so a live-in nanny was mandatory for us.

All went well, but we were crazy busy. I began coaching and doing some choreography for Dorothy. She needed guidance as all athletes do, especially for the competitive tricks she performed in the shows. It was all about keeping her sharp.

Juanita came home very often. She also did three Hamill television shows and special appearances with Dorothy. In that crowd we were exposed to many fun, famous people. Juanita nicknamed Dorothy "Squint," because she had trouble seeing sometimes without her glasses. We had her date Desi Arnaz Jr. for publicity purposes. Then she ended up dating Dean Martin Jr., her first true love. We had their private engagement party at our place. Dean was so much fun and was now actively pursuing his tennis career. He made two movies and was always bringing fun people to our home like Andy Gibb, David Cassidy, Desi, Billy Hinsche, and Wilt Chamberlain, who was Juanita's friend from the early days. Then in 1979 my student Lynn Holly Johnson, a national novice skater, made the feature movie "Ice Castles" which I worked on for Columbia Pictures. What fun! So between coaching the Korean Champion for the Olympics and Tai and Randy and the celebrities, we were jumping! All was falling into place and Los Angeles was our mecca.

The L.A./Hollywood bug bit Tasha and Juanita. Tasha was totally involved in modeling and pursued acting for a few years at the ripe old age of 10. Agent Artis Burton represented her and Juanita chauffeured her to something like 200 auditions, a few of which proved to be successful. It was a great experience for both of them.

We started to go to award shows like the American Comedy Awards as VIPs. We were also going to Dean and Jennie Martin's home in Beverly Hills, and to parties with Phyllis Diller, astronaut John Glenn, Rod Stewart and a host of others. We were very active now. Our beautiful experience with Dorothy helped us mature and opened life's doors. We worked and played and parented hard, and this continued for five years. Dorothy was always giving, gracious and close to us and our girls, and I love her for that to this day.

Be The Launchpad For Your Children — To Grow

The Ice Capades Chalet rink was becoming the mecca magnet for top amateur national and international skaters, and because we were owned by the world-famous Ice Capades, top professional performers would train with us during their "off" seasons. The wanna-be little starlets who were not really good enough to win championships but did have the "it" performance factor hung around like flies to try to get the chance for a professional audition to join the traveling ice show. Now in the summer of 1976, Dorothy Hamill signed with Michael Rosenburg, then later with agent Jerry Weintraub, and a very lucrative financial contract where Ice Capades would tour her in 21 major cities. Dorothy came to L.A., the main headquarters for Ice Capades. The company felt she was the "Golden Girl" of the decade and that we must keep her happy at all costs. After all, she was the big drawing card. I was thrilled to be able to help her. We continued our coaching relationship for almost six years and she remains dear to my heart today.

Worlds in Vienna, Austria, in 1977 and I was there with my new little family as an assistant coach for Tai and Randy. So crazy me, in the locker room area during the final results of the Men's Championship; the red carpet was laid and podium set, with fans on pins and needles waiting for the announcement. I grabbed hometown boys Wolfgang Schwarz and Emmerich Danzer and said, "Guys, let's have some fun and run out NOW, stand on the podium just as we did 10 years ago, here!" They looked at me confused and chickened out. Too bad, as it could have been a real ABC moment. I am sure the arena audience would have gone wild.

Living Examples Are Few And Far Between

By 1980 Tai and Randy were already 1979 World Champions and set for the Olympic Gold. Mr. Nicks and I stood at the ice rail in Canada that wonderful moment together when they became first in the world. I was so very proud for him and his victory; I was able to help and he made me feel such a part of it all. It was a growing moment in my pro career.

The 1980 Olympics in Lake Placid were devastating for Tai and Randy. After finishing the short program Randy suffered an injury and had to withdraw from the Championship and retire without the chance for Olympic Gold. We were all devastated.

I remember that summer, Robin Cousins (1980 Olympic Men's Champion) stayed at our home for a while. We had a cute, funny little dog named Poo Bear. That dog fell in love with Robin and would wake him every morning after sneaking into his room and grabbing onto his right leg and not letting go. It was a doggie love affair for sure. Thus we nicknamed Robin "Poodie," a title he bears today that he will never live down.

In late 1980 the training center was sold by Ice Capades as the land in Santa Monica was just too valuable. I moved in September of that year after the 1980 Olympics in Lake Placid, where I had won my first U.S. title 15 years earlier. I moved with 14 national and elite skaters to Culver City, a small city only seven miles from the Santa Monica Chalet. There I developed local, regional, national and international skaters through the 2010 Olympics in Vancouver. The World scene also happened in 2009 in Los Angeles when I was a coach and team leader and had a skater representing India on the world stage. Then at the 2010 Olympics Taka Kozuka (Japan) placed eighth, and in

2011 second at Worlds. Working with him in summers, I felt rewarded by his results.

Along with the obligations of head coach, the benefits came, and my personal school there thrived. This was now my home rink and was just bought by the L.A. Kings ice hockey team as their practice rink when the huge Forum Stadium Arena was not available. Through their presence at our arena, I became involved in coaching power stroking for hockey players. We had our 360-member youth hockey program and I conducted special skating for speed, power and agility for our young hockey teams. Through that program four of my private lesson boys made the National Hockey League, two went to skate for European professional teams, and one girl became a two-time U.S. Women's Olympic Hockey Team Captain. How proud am I! She was under my tutelage since she was very very young.

The L.A. Kings used me to work with some of their players on weak skating points — players like Luc Robitaille, Doug Smith and several others — during the off season. Other NHL players also came through my program from various NHL teams all over North America.

We also did a video, "The Other Side of Hockey," on advanced power stroking. This lead to an offer to direct, organize, and choreograph an ESPN one-hour television special on the debut of the new Ducks NHL hockey team, and put together and audition and choreograph the new concept of ice cheerleaders, the "Decoys," 12 beautiful ice queens to electrify the fans between periods and at the opening of every game. Disney Corporation President Michael Eisner was the contact who asked me and I worked long and hard and was extremely pleased with the television special and our beautiful 12 Decoy cheerleaders. I coached the Eisner boys in private power skating lessons and had a great rapport with Mr. Eisner, his wife Jane and the two boys.

My name was filtering into pro ice hockey circles and my opportunities broadened to an area that was new and challenging for me. I do remember training, from 1964 to 1966, in Detroit with the Red Wings at the Old Olympia Stadium, running around the ice there with Gordie Howe and the team while they finished their drills. I was given the ice for two hours to train for the World Championships. This was, I guess, my inspiration for my 120 power ice drills that I developed for my teaching program. I enjoyed a diverse career at this arena for over 33 wonderful years until late 2012.

The 1984 Olympics in Sarajevo, Yugoslavia, proved historic for figure skating — 18 marks of 6.0 for one performance — the perfect score in skating. Most of us champions have received 5.9s and once or twice a perfect score. I did at the World Professional Championships at Wembley Stadium in 1969; a perfect score for "overall performance." Torvill and Dean were Olympic Dance Champions and they alone hold that unbelievable moment in the history of the sport. Eighteen 6.0s! Fantastic.

The Bigger The Challenge The Stronger The Effort

I was with friend and fellow skater Scott Hamilton the evening he won the Gold at those 1984 games. He skated extremely well in the final long, but not his best. We had all finished the press conference and were on the athlete's bus going back to the Olympic Village. I was there because I lived with the athletes as team leader and coach for the Korean skating team. Scott was confiding in me and complaining, "I didn't skate my best, I am so disappointed." It was that perfection thing again that we all have in sports.

I said, "Okay, Scott. I'll give you the most spectacular performance of your life, but you have to change that gold medal hanging around your neck for a silver."

He looked at me and smiled, then nodded, "Okay, I get it."

Then I said, "It doesn't say in the record book that you skated great or poorly, it states that you were first. Gold." You never have to apologize to anyone, ever.

Goals Are Meant For Growth

For many seasons after his final Olympic win Scott trained with me every summer and on tour breaks in Los Angeles. He remains a dear friend to this day, a great man and athlete, a true Olympic hero and a gentleman.

I do remember one week Scott stayed with us (Juanita and I) in our home. Little Michele was then about nine and had the large bedroom with the extra bed, so Scott shared her room. One morning he got up late, about 8:30, and was laughing. He had a note in his hand. He explained that he had left Michele a nice note two days earlier asking her to please not rock in her bed at night. She answered him back in a special note, "I'll stop rocking if you stop farting." What a pair! We laugh about it to this day.

As reluctant as my father was about my starting skating, Juanita and I kept saying no to our Michele and her constant requests to start gymnastics. Our reasons were very different from my Dad. We knew how difficult and time consuming this "no future" sport was and

143

we also knew (given her parent's backgrounds) that she could become very good. We were selfish and held her start for some three years. At age 10 she jumped in late. Michele flourished in California and by 13 moved on her own to a large academy in Utah, and lived with the head coach and his family. Two seasons later she went to Bela Karolyi in Texas. She trained on his elite team for a while. At his request, I flew to meet him and he told me that because of her late start there were some severe shortcomings, which we already knew. The 1988 Seoul Olympics were 10 months away and she would not make the top 15 in America. Michele said, "Dad, let's go home."

I said okay and then she said, "Dad, I wanted to become and Olympian like you."

I answered with a tearful eye, "You are an Olympian person. Let's go, we can all be together again."

She never spoke of that five years of her life ever again. Sports gave her so much strength, will, and discipline, which carries her through life today. She did utilize her talented gym form for a national commercial which aired for almost a year.

I now have a little star, one working and pushing and guiding toward local victories. He was about eight years old and a fierce, fast, fun hockey player. He was a crazy little Evel Knievel on blades. I took an instant liking to his freedom and abandonment. He was fearless. His mom was totally dedicated to her son and usually hard to deal with, although she and I always managed to compromise. She wanted me to improve his speed and power and maybe introduce him to figure skating. Trifun Zivanovic, an unusual name. His dad was Yugoslavian and I really admired his hard work ethic from the old country, and his mom Glenda was always extremely supportive and would do anything to help her son. His passion for hockey was tremendous.

Trif and I bonded over the years and I always felt, even early on, that he could be on the U.S. World Team and skate in the Olympics. He didn't fail me or himself. He became second in America, skated five World Championships, and one Olympics. How very proud he made me, every year of our 28 years of coach-student relationship.

Probably the most memorable program Trif is noted for would no doubt be "West Side Story." Choreographing his character as lead "Jet" gang leader, I really tried to use and embellish his free and "street-like" style, and it worked. My favorite piece he and I did was "The Rocketeer." It was so "on" and made for jumps and spins and speed. He truly jumped like a rocket man.

It was a great journey. Even though his mom did take him away from me three different times, I respected her so much. She was so dedicated to him and his career. We were very close friends until her death in 2010. A real straight shooter, and Trifun was her reason for living, always.

He was truly my product and he was so talented and never gave up. I am so proud of him, always, even today, and we remain close friends.

Life Is An Adventure, Share While You Can

Our "Ice Sickies" home video: me, Dean Martin Jr. and Juanita.

Me and Kristi Yamaguchi.

Following Page:

Top: Me and Dorothy Hamill at my home in 1977.

Bottom: Working with the boys: Elvis Stojko and Brian Boitano

Los Angeles, 1984 Summer Olympics. Wow, we started really working to host the best 16 days in Olympic sport. History does state the financial success of the games in Los Angeles. For the first time the Olympic games produced a surplus — a $364 million dollar surplus. As a local Southern California Olympian I acted as one of the senior "Spirit Team" public speakers, promoting and educating our community and state to prepare for, host and cherish the Olympic moment. Dr. Andy Strenk, swimmer, Olympian and my friend, became the right arm and a true worker dedicated to Peter Ueberroth, the head commissioner of our games. L.A. did put in the best, most comprehensive bid for the games to the IOC (International Olympic Committee). Andy worked 24/7 for two years and I was honored to help all I could to make his job easier and to bring together over 60 local organizations to unite for our cause. The U.S.A. (under President Carter) had boycotted the 1980 Summer Olympics in Russia because of the Russian invasion of Afghanistan or whatever, so the Olympic spirit was keen.

Our athletes were biting at the bit to compete in Los Angeles. Russia was ready to boycott, and did. Momentum grew in Southern California faster than the facilities could be built. Californians were excited and supportive of the Games. This was the first time corporate America was firmly behind any Olympics, so the international scene was watching closely as to how we Americans would do with this new concept. Usually the national government would put up funds to support the Games. Well, history was made. L.A. was 110 percent successful. The newly found "Spirit Team" was a tremendous energizer toward universal acceptance and community involvement. The L.A. Olympics were privately funded and we made money for the first time ever. Los Angeles showed the world that the Olympics can stand on its own and be financially sound.

As the Olympic flame faded, the work to continue the Olympic movement in California continued. The Amateur Athletic Foundation was formed and funded by the $364 million dollar surplus after the Games. My dear friend Anita DeFrantz, Olympian and fellow Spirit Team member, was named AAF President. She has built the best and most comprehensive sports museum and sports library in the world, based in Los Angeles. My hat is off to her and the AAF; she is a rock, and became an IOC member.

Now Olympians in California are really on the sport map! Our alumni organization was just getting pulled together after the 1984 Games and I was voted in as president of the Southern California Olympians. I had to organize, communicate with and use 2,800 registered elite athletes to continue to grow the post-Olympic movement. I helped build the Spirit Team speakers' bureau so athletes could give inspirational speeches in schools, hospitals, senior citizen centers, etc. and be a strong lobbying force within political circles local and statewide. And believe me, there were issues and movements to bring to the public's attention.

Sitting as president of this diverse group of outstanding people, I used my office headquarters at the fantastic Amateur Athletic Foundation — along with board meetings, special events and the help of their executive staff — to help promote the alumni.

So many wonderful opportunities came my way as alumni president over so many years. In 1987, Arnold Schwarzenegger formed a coalition of "Actors for Bush," and I then organized "Athletes for Bush" as Arnold and I joined forces. George H.W. Bush was running a new campaign and we met with his people in California and pledged to be with the Vice President whenever and wherever he campaigned in our state. Jointly, Arnold and I promoted and attended some six rallies for Mr. Bush. At the election he carried California and it helped him to win.

Juanita and I were invited to Washington for the Inauguration on January 21, 1988. At The Kennedy Center and Ball, Juanita and I had a fantastic experience. I used the days there to meet several people in the new administration. Within six weeks I had a Presidential appointment; I so graciously accepted and went through the extensive paperwork and thorough background checks. There was an unmarked black car sitting in front of my home in Beverly Hills on Spaulding Drive for five days! They really checked us out. After all, we would be with the President of the United States. Arnold was asked to be the Commissioner of the President's Council on Physical Fitness and Sports, a commission and agency founded by President Kennedy in 1961. It's main function was to monitor, control, and set standards for school fitness and physical education requirements, and oversee the President's "Sports Awards Program" too.

By March 1988 we were meeting for the first time in Washington, D.C., and the new members were Arnold, fellow Olympian and friend Peter Vidmar, and myself, along with 10 existing members. I understood that many fellow Americans were considered and I was extremely honored to have been chosen among so many qualified individuals who were in consideration ... more than 250 people.

I remember being driven through the security gates and thinking "what a house." How many really powerful people have lived here? Visited here? It is America's house: the White House. This was my first visit to meet the President. I could only envision my Mom ironing clothes many years ago and being so upset about my U.S. Army draft induction notice. This was during the height of my competitive career some 22 years ago. What would she have thought of me now? She had called this place to object to the President about her son, a National Champion, being inducted into the Army. Mom passed away in 1982.

Our new mission was Daily Quality Physical Education in the school systems, this at a time when schools were cutting budgets and math and science teachers were forced to sit in during P.E. classes. Obesity in children was escalating and senior citizens had no role models or avenues to bring quality to their golden years.

Arnold was a star, a real attraction in America, and he was a very clever businessman. My office at the ice rink was only four miles from his office in Santa Monica, which was a real advantage. I would go at least two mornings each week for several hours and work very closely with his voice and right arm man, George Otott, a former military lifer who knew fitness in America like the back of his hand and everyone who made it move and shake, like advisor John Cates.

Awareness was key and Arnold could bring that to the people ... the movers and the shakers as well as "Joe citizen." Everyone loved Arnold; after all, he was the Terminator, our hero, self-made and married into the Kennedy family! He shined, he asked, and he received! He owned the decade.

We traveled so many times together: Fitness fairs, seminars, huge statewide conferences, national conferences in Washington, D.C., and all over America.

Is It Your Human Obligation To Help Others? Yes!

Arnold was asked to speak at the opening ceremonies of the 1990 Goodwill Games in Seattle, Washington. He was always so interested in top sportsmen and was excited to go. He had a good six-minute speech ready, which Maria helped him with. He had me fly up with him in his plane — a 2-1/2-hour flight — and I made him practice the speech 15 times. "Slow, pause, take your time ... remember it is an outside stadium and the sound will echo or vibrate, so speak slowly and with less accent, too!" I am sure he was ready to kill me. He did slow down and listen, and performed well.

We were in the presence of Governor Booth Gardner at a press photo opportunity at the gym in the stadium. Arnold was so attentive to the workout machines and helping and guiding. Afterwards we showered and got ready for the opening ceremonies.

On our way up to our seats in the backstage tunnel a guy was sitting on a crate playing the flute. He said, "Hey, hi Arnold," and Arnold smiled back.

We walked a little further and I said, "Hey, that was Kenny G." Arnold looked puzzled but said "Cool."

We were sitting in our seats waiting for the ceremonies to start. The stadium was full, and sitting in front of Arnold and I were Jane Fonda and Ted Turner, and next to me was Mr. Armand Hammer. I saw that on the large Jumbotron television screens as they were panning for celebrities in the audience. I also noticed that the camera was approaching Jane and Ted Turner, ready to focus on us. He was wiping his nose with his hand and at that moment I pushed his hand down. He was startled but recognized what was going down and smiled at the big screen. Mr. Hammer waved and I said, "So, you're a ham."

He laughed and said, "I got a new pacemaker installed last week and don't have to change it for 10 years, they said!" Now he was already like 82 ... what a character!

So now we are at the VIP reception. Arnold was really enjoying himself and fortunately everyone came up to him to say hello, from ambassadors to politicians. I knew their names and prompted him so he could address them personally. Arnold was impressed. I was just lucky to remember. We even got to meet and greet President Reagan that night and when we were in the reception line of eight people, Arnold turned to me and asked, "How do you want me to introduce you to the President? How about my Fancy Figure Skating Friend from the Fifties?" That was his usual joke.

I said, "If you do I will kick you so hard!"

Well, at that moment the President was extending his hand to Arnold, they spoke, then Arnold turned to me and said, "Mr. President ..." He hesitated, and I was sweating it! But then he introduced me properly and all was calm. He really had me for a moment. Crazy kidder, he is, always, but I love him for that.

Life Can Be Magical ... Make Sure That You Are A Part Of It

So it's like 6:20 a.m. and I am on the ice coaching and my cell phone rings in my pocket and for some reason I answered it. The voice was deep and it was obviously Arnold.

"Gary? It's Arnold."

"I know it's you. Who the hell else says my name with that accent?"

He ignored that and said, "I've been up all night, recording with Guns N' Roses for the movie score."

I said, "Well, whatever you do don't quit your acting job for singing, because you suck." He laughed, and then I said, "Wow, you must be bored to call me at six in the morning."

He asked, "What are you doing?"

"Working, what do you think? I can't play like you and earn millions."

These spontaneous calls I will always cherish, and I'll never try to figure him out. I'll just be there for him, as he would for me.

Whatever You Can Imagine You Can Create

Inspiring: Arnold. He is! So one Christmas he sent me a book. The book — my book — the stimulating revelation ... open my mind book ... the real thing! He signed and wrote, "A Merry Christmas and a Healthy New Year. Thank you for helping make America a fitter and healthier nation. Your Good Friend, Arnold, 1992," with a smiley face. Well, this was my kickoff to write some things on my own. The book is "Great Quotes from Great Leaders." How powerful. Arnold, you set me off and running with my thoughts and pen. My sincere gratitude for that my longtime friend!

The second great push from Arnold: Just before Bill Clinton came into office in January of 1992, President Bush and 12 of us said our goodbyes in the oval office. When we left that afternoon we were completing our special Presidential appointment now that Bush was leaving. Talking with Arnold, he suggested that I start my own "Movement for Fitness" in California. So his push and inspiration moved me forward to organize and found the "United Fitness Foundation" using local Olympians. We had fitness fairs at schools and gave inspirational health speeches at some 110 schools from 1992 to 1999. Thanks Arnold, for that.

Can I Really Contribute To Humanity?

I have been blessed to have been associated with many prominent people, celebrities, and movers and shakers alike. The most influential and lasting relationship has been with Arnold. It's funny because we have few mutual friends but somehow a connection was always there. He is a complicated man, but yet real simple. He knows where he is and where he was from, with a real direction always toward his next challenge. A fun loving, joking, take charge, do well sort of man who is extremely brilliant. He knows how to bring people together, direct them and bring out their best to accomplish a goal. Then he will move on from there. My five-year working relationship with him was a time I will always cherish and remember. Getting things done, bringing people together, and having a worldwide perspective are a few of the qualities I developed through his example and guidance. A little arrogant, yet understanding and confident in areas he was first stepping into ... with top people and situations never before traveled. Keep it simple (the message and purpose), and repeat the slogan. He would always tell me, "Go for it!" and, "You got it!" Thank you, Arnold, for being in my life.

The Gifts You Can't Purchase Have More Value

The mid-1990s were a time of loss again. More than 15 of my former male students and friends died of AIDS. Also, I was now facing the slow death of my relationship with my best friend and wife.

After almost 25 years of marriage (the girls were 20 and 25), Juanita and I decided to part. She desperately needed to be Juanita Percelly again. Mrs. Gary Visconti was not where her happiness was any longer. She needed to be out on her own. She had just secured a good position working for my friend Hiro Yamagata (a world famous Japanese artist) and so she felt she could take care of herself. The girls were out of the house now and finding their own worlds. All separation and divorces, I wish, should go as smooth as ours did — really respectful and easy. There was a tremendous loss and a huge feeling of failure. Everyone had said 25 years ago, "It will never last." That haunted me for a while, and I worked so hard to let that go. It took time and much effort, for both of us. I was single and a little lost for over a year. Thank God for work.

After my divorce, my girls were in college and out working and I needed some real "Gary time." I started going to Cabo San Lucas, Mexico, because one of my client's families had a condo on the beach in a resort setting and offered use of it to me. I jumped at the chance and the flight was very reasonable and only two hours from Los Angeles. And, our rink was just 15 minutes from the airport. Pre-911, there was no real security at the airport, and easy access. I must have gone some 40 visits, about once every five weeks for at least seven years; a great getaway for me and a new life of freedom with new faces and places. I love Mexico and its culture.

Then, only 11 months later, Mr. Don went into the hospital for a minor operation but had trouble breathing in recovery because he smoked so much. The doctor kept him there for 48 hours and he had a breathing tube down his throat. He tore it out twice ... what a strong and stubborn man. I flew back twice to Phoenix that week to assure him that all would be fine and that he was not permanently on any machine or lifesaving device. That last night I left he tore the tube out again and died. He was only about 64. I felt part of me died that day. With all that happened, Mr. Don's death was so very unnecessary and earth-shaking for me.

I felt so very guilty because it was me who encouraged him wholeheartedly to do that minor surgery in the first place. Was it my fault? The guilt with that was with me for six months, but I finally was at peace with it all when I buried him back in Michigan with his beloved parents.

Back in L.A. and working on my coaching career, I had several top skaters to attend to and Trifun was heading for the National Junior Title. Mr. Don remains in my heart and thoughts daily, and always will. He truly was the wind beneath my wings, my daily inspiration to succeed, and the driving force to victory. I thank him daily for believing in me and never giving up on our quest. He was my hero in so many ways. Part of me died with him. He showed me so many positive ingredients to work life to its fullest, to be strong, independent, focused and self-confident.

Never Fear You Will be Forgotten, Because You Are Written In The Stars

Decade 6: Teaching

Teach: 1a: to cause to know something <taught them a trade> b: to cause to know how <is teaching me to drive> c: to accustom to some action or attitude <teach students to think for themselves> 2: to guide the studies of; 3: to impart the knowledge of 4a: to instruct by precept, example, or experience b: to make known and accepted <experience teaches us our limitations>
— Webster's Dictionary

Teaching ... At the age where you have gained a vast amount of experience fermented in wisdom, you must learn how to convey all of that earned knowledge to many different listeners, at many different levels, in many different ways. Know that your experience combined with theirs will eventually shape who they are and the course they take. Example is always the best, most effective way to teach and to impress those lost participants in life; share and nurture.
— Gary Visconti

Sometimes I can't believe I'm a teacher, a coach. As a kid growing up, I was someone who couldn't focus in a classroom. I was restless. I was disinterested. I listened to very little but I noticed everything. School was difficult for me and I'm sure that at least two learning disabilities — dyslexia and Attention Deficit Disorder — were prevalent within me and messing with my head. Being left handed didn't help in my daily life, either. But, I think to be a great teacher you have to go through it yourself; you have to overcome the obstacles so that you can help others with empathy and understanding and wisdom. You have to be willing to learn ... always, endlessly, forever.

In my case, it seemed like I always had to learn things the hard way. If I was not interested in something or if I didn't want to do it, well, then I would become very stubborn and disengaged. However, if I really loved something (like art) or if I felt challenged (i.e. my skating) then I competed hard and flourished big time. My mother told me later in life that I had the uncanny ability to concentrate on one thing and block out the world. She said, "You could read a book sitting in the middle of the freeway if you wanted."

As a child I always had interests, of course, but just not what the adults had in mind. I feel that a good parent nurtures and promotes and cultivates the things in which their child is interested in, not what they themselves are interested in for their child. This approach, I have found, also helps in the bonding between child and parent, not to mention the confidence a child gains by knowing that their parents are in their corner. As adults, we can learn a great deal from youth and, in turn, if we pick our high ground properly, we can teach them a better perspective and to value so many aspects of life that we had to learn.

We Can Learn Big Lesson From Little People

I learned so much when my Dad passed away. I was 66 years old. Dad was a rock. Ninety-four-and-a-half and strong and wise to the end. Death is such a part of life, and somehow we all avoid talking about it or sharing feelings with family prior to that dreaded event. Our outlook and concept of "permanently relocating" to somewhere no one has ever come back from inspires fear. I am sure that no one has come back because it is better. We should share with all family members our feelings and our own reality of death. I feel it is healthy to discuss and share something so profound, and eventually we all must face it.

Perfect — No. Persistence — Yes!

I do remember standing on the ice listening to Mr. Don instructing me on some crazy ice move and having no earthly idea what the hell he was talking about. I would never let him know it, but instead chose to always give it a whirl even though I had no understanding of the concept. And, you know what — it always worked out! That man knew what he was talking about and the lesson learned for me was to just do what the master said and, in that exercise of working it out, I would "get it" eventually. Mr. Don once told me, "Gary, do you know why you are the best? Do you know what has made you a champion? It wasn't your talent because there are plenty of more talented skaters out there. And, it sure wasn't my coaching because half the time I didn't know what I was doing. I had to study skating manuals and watch movies of older champions to keep two steps ahead of you. First reason: You let me coach you. Second reason: You never, ever gave up. The one thing that really separates you out and defines you is this: I could literally tell you to go practice a move until you get it right and you would, every time. Forty, 50 falls, hours at a time, bloody knees; it didn't matter. You would do what I asked of you and you would never quit until you got it right."

So many lessons there: Trust, determination, "never-say-die" attitude, a "no quit" approach. Persistence. It's about listening, learning and perfecting.

Not ... Can I Conquer; How Can I?

To convey a message, we must always know who we are speaking to. In my sports coaching, my students have ranged from 4-1/2 years old to 76 years young. This huge age span kept me on my toes and was a constant challenge to my communicative creativity and my ability to get results instantly (hopefully), at some level.

With All The Communication Devices In The World Today, Man Still Cannot Communicate

On Teaching ...

To convey an idea or concept does take skill and my skills are always getting better. There are always several ways to deliver your message. The oldest form of communication is the spoken word but sometimes it can be challenging to get someone else to understand you or even pay attention for any length of time. Some of my students were 61 years younger than me and, boy, can that be an obstacle if I let it become one. I just put myself in their shoes and try to see through their limited sight line, and explain my theory in a concept they can relate to and, thus, understand. For them, visualization through relatable stories usually works best. I try to keep the student in their "mental environment" in order to help them better picture the concept. I try to keep away from technical terms, whenever possible, and the KISS (Keep It Simple Stupid) method always seems to best explain the point, or truth, I am trying to make. My teaching advice: Don't "over talk" the issue but, instead, let your student ask the questions. And listen ... listen so that you can work the lesson or conversation to a proper conclusion so they can fully wrap their minds around your theory or concept. Remember, everyone has different levels of acceptance, understanding and vision. Not everyone sees things in the same way, or at the same speed. The main goal is to get them to grasp the concept and learn the skill in their own way. It is about them, achieving for them.

I had the pleasure of giving many international skating seminars. The few that stand out were those in Australia, Japan, and South Korea. The host skating federations were generous to me; in fact, attendance for the three-day schools was overbooked. I returned several years in a row. The communication skills I learned and lasting friendships are worth their weight in gold. As for working through the language barriers ... thank God for the interpreters!

There Are As Many Ideas Of Heaven As There Are People On Earth

Don't Take Your Knowledge And Experience With You

I tried daily with all of my students of any age to share one little word of wisdom or new thought with them just to get them thinking outside of their box and listening to me! They didn't always understand but I keep throwing those "new" thoughts out there and up in the air hoping that I have introduced them to a concept that they may later engage, and find answers to, or help in their time of need. In turn, my students challenged me constantly and kept me thinking ... young and on my toes, too! Their perception of life and times and situations were always surprising to me. I learned, too, about them always.

"I can't communicate with these kids." As a teacher, coach and mentor, you never feel like they really "get it." I continually — daily, hourly — just put myself in their shoes. Mr. Don was only 14 years older than me. Now, I am like 50 years older than my students. I have to think young, daily, to keep in tune, keep current, and communicate.

Experience The Difference Good Thoughts Can Make

The "word," spoken or written, is a very powerful thing. It can change people's outlooks and, in turn, change the world in an instant. Just think, we all have the power to "move" a person emotionally and intellectually with our words. Sometimes, just a word. A kind word can uplift a spirit and a compliment can restore and heal. A harsh word can deflate and hateful speech can tear down and destroy. These reactions can make a lifelong impression on young people, and they remember.

"Mr. Gary, I want you to know I bought your autograph on eBay last week. Can I bring it in and you tell me if it is really yours from 1967?" said one of my young students about two years ago.

I answered, "You didn't have to pay for it, I could have just signed one now." It was authentic, and I didn't ask how much she spent on eBay for it, which was probably a good thing!

I have been so blessed to live in an era when great people dared to speak great truths. Some I will always remember, and have truly influenced me:

- President Franklin Delano Roosevelt spoke truth into the hearts of an entire nation when he said, "The only thing we have to fear is fear itself."
- President John F. Kennedy challenged the entire electorate with his, "Ask not what your country can do for you but what you can do for your country."
- Rev. Martin Luther King lifted the spirits of an entire race of citizenry when he dared to say, "I have a dream ... that the measure of a man is not judged by the color of his skin but by the content of his character."
- And, President Ronald Reagan boldly dared the Cold War Eastern European powers to, "Tear down this wall, Mr. Gorbachev!" Yes, take down any wall that may inhibit you and your growth.

Common Sense Is Not So Common

Of course, the concept of "change" is usually not fully realized when it comes to individual people. I mean, we can sometimes help to alter an individual's attitude through some course correction but, in general, people pretty much stay the same from childhood. My fun, nice, old friends from my very early years are still fun and nice. The mean and ugly attitude kids are still the same at age 65. People, in general, get a little bit better or a little bit worse but basically they remain the same; it's always their choice to change or not. You can lead any of us to water but you can't make us drink. I had the advantage of good, honest, caring parents and great mentors along the way. Not everyone is so lucky and fortunate as I have been. Some of the people who most influenced my life were:

To Listen Is Golden — To Understand, Harmony

- President John F. Kennedy (I was 18 to 21 years old during his presidency)
- Coach Pierre Brunet
- Coach John Nicks
- Coach Bud Wilson
- Coach Gus Lussi
- Schoolteacher Rosemary Kluffman
- Aunt Jenny Facchini
- My Mom and Dad, of course
- Coach Don
- Arnold Schwarzenegger
- President George H.W. Bush
- Doug Ramsey
- Skate Judge Arnold Schroeder
- Skate Judge Teddy Rittenger
- Mr. F. Ritter Shumway
- Dick T. Button
- David Jenkins
- Carol Heiss Jenkins

And so many, many more. You each taught me something through word and deed and example ... and I watched and listened, and remember.

A Smile Is A Stranger's Hug

On Friendships ...

A true friend, a real lifelong friend, doesn't really need to ask if you need help or if they need to be around — they just do and they just are ... always there for you. They are like eagles — never fly in flocks. To the contrary, advice is something that should always only be asked for before being offered. My Mom used to say, "Never give advice because the smart people don't need it and the dumb people don't heed it."

Advice is something that should be asked for first, then given, because someone who is asking really wants to know and the person not asking thinks they already know. Be a good listener. Let the other people talk then echo back to them what they said. Their answer, idea, or path will then become self-evident and self-directed. It's a win-win scenario and will cut down on the hard feelings in the friendship and help avoid conflict and misunderstandings.

Following Page:
Top: Coaching Frank Gerhy
Bottom: Me and Jerry Bruckheimer

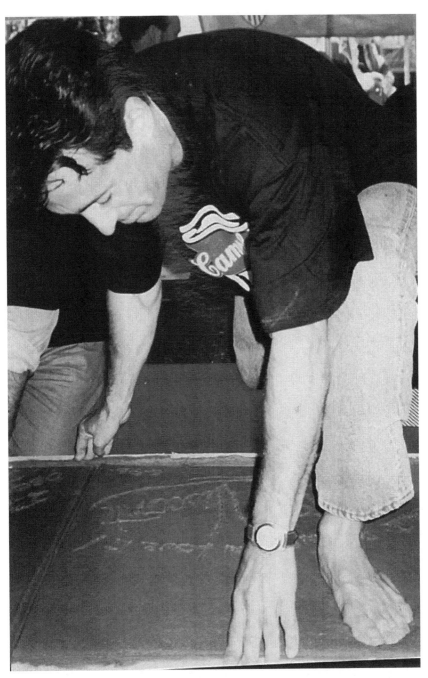

Leaving my mark at the Hall of Fame in Colorado Springs, Colorado.

With Meg Ryan!

Following Page
Top: Me and Trifun Zivanovic celebrating his first place finish in
Germany
Bottom: Skating friends gather at the Olympians salute event.

Celebrating together at the World Hall of Fame.

World Championship send-off party of Trifun.

Teaching Clarisse Garcia at my home ice arena.

I have been so blessed to have some of the best friends, some for over 50 years. Somewhere during the 1994 calendar my office phone rang and the voice on the other end said, "Mr. Gehry wishes to speak to you." I thought to myself, "Who?" and was subsequently asked by this Mr. Gehry if I would take on his two sons, Aligo and Sammie, for power hockey instruction. He added that he heard I was the best around and, after questioning him about the boys, arrangements were finalized. The boys were cool, fun kids who were eager to learn. About two years later, the foremost architect in the world, the internationally renowned Frank Gehry, became a client of mine for two reasons. First, he wanted to have some fun time with his boys. Second, Frank had been asked, as an international celebrity, to take part in some charity hockey games up in Canada and he really didn't want to embarrass himself in front of 15,000 people. We developed a great relationship and his twice weekly lessons became a fun and rewarding time for both of us for years.

Later, after going through the L.A. Disney Hall Project and all the ups and downs, triumphs and tragedies that it encompassed, Frank said to me, "You know, Gary, my new design concepts of curved, flowing buildings comes from you and skating. I took what you showed to me and explained to me about the blade edges of skates on the ice and all of the curve and turn techniques and I incorporated them into my new designs." That really blew me away. How cool is that?

Now, at age 84, Frank is still a wonderful friend, a stellar man, and so very constant in our ever-changing world; a true legend. I am so proud to be his friend. I remember when I got my first loft in Venice, California, and he and his wife Berta came over for dinner and later wanted to get me a housewarming gift. I told him that I loved the new chairs he designed, made in Germany, with the woven wood slats called "Cross Check" — an ice hockey term. Wouldn't you know it, four weeks later the chairs arrived at my home. I was one happy guy. I later found out that he had to personally purchase the chairs for me and have them shipped from Germany. Such a gracious man and I later had him sign the chairs for me. They remain one of my prized possessions to this day.

During the same period I was contracted by the incredible filmmaker and producer Jerry Bruckheimer. He too is an avid ice hockey fan and player, so much so that he has a huge yearly hockey weekend in Las Vegas with professional and semi-professional players. I had the pleasure of being a small part of his life for over 15 years, twice weekly coaching him privately on the ice. He opened my eyes to the complexity of filmmaking a made me privy to some of the glitz and glitter. We are both from Detroit, from the same generation and with the same values. He is truly a hard-working and humble man of great talent and drive. Thanks for all you exposed me to in the film world.

A rock of a P.R. woman, she was there for me always for 20 years. Sharon Jimenez, wife of four-time Emmy Award winner for live journalism Bob Jimenez, has been relentless for huge political causes such as gerrymandering in California, two presidential campaigns, independence for Hollywood as a city, and co-founder (with me) of the Bring Hollywood Home Foundation, a 501c4 promoting statewide public awareness of movie outsourcing and encouraging independent film producers to be properly funded and to film in California. By no means a small task, this met with huge opposition by large movie corporations and related associations. As CEO, Sharon worked tirelessly with a passion for fairness and unsurpassed opportunities for young lost filmmakers to receive fundraising, fairly and deservedly to fulfill their dreams and enhance society.

Being A Parent Is Not Apparent To Everyone

On Parenting ...

The best method of teaching is always by example; actions speak so much louder than words. Children, especially, learn from watching, not hearing. Think about it ... video games, smartphones and computers are so fascinating to the younger set and they really don't talk as much as they watch and react. These newer generations are visual, texting, etc., all the way. So, how do you teach your child not to smoke or drink or eat poorly if you do? Teach through the example of lifestyle. Your courtesy to others, personal hygiene, attention to health and fitness, even your eating and sleeping habits must all be exhibited daily, consistently, constantly. This is the most effective, non-invasive teaching style and tool — living by example. Be strong and firm but deliver the message gently through the visual of your own daily life. These core values can never be taught late in life and should not be replaced. The first five years are key.

I had a strong, honest, old school, salt-of-the-earth Dad who had correct values at the very root of himself. He led by example ... and a few chosen words ... but he instilled in his kids a real strong core of beliefs. A lot of family heritage from Milan, Italy, came here through him. He was religious, hard-working and conservative without being too judgmental. He lived his own style of life daily, consistently, and loved it. Always on a regular schedule, Dad was all about family first and seemingly never "wanted" for himself. He was very sharp, always had his eyes wide open, and checked then rechecked everything. All of these honest real values were taught to me by my parent's example and I am forever grateful for them. I carry them with me constantly, lovingly, respectfully.

Fast forward to today's society where the more "intelligent" the world becomes, the more work and thinking that is done for you. And, we have become a dimmer, dumber people as a result. It seems like we Americans are now "hot house tomatoes" where we can only thrive if conditions are perfect. Well, there is no such thing as "perfect" and the more you know for yourself, the more you can do for yourself, the more adaptable and flexible and equipped you will be to handle life's ever-changing imperfections and interruptions. Our success, as a people and as individuals, will be determined by our flexibility, core values, and ability to overcome and adapt to a new world — daily! We must learn how to survive and thrive in and amongst all the changes and curves thrown our way. Remember, we are constantly being tested every day in every way by our own selves, others, nature, and life in general. So keep your strong feet well planted in the soil and respect heritage and nature, but be ready for change.

If I Have Grown From My Mistakes, Then I Am Now Nine Feet Three Inches Tall

On Finding Yourself ...

So, to truly find yourself and your way in this world, you need to "work" on yourself. How do you do that? Well, for starters, tune in to your own wants, desires, needs and shortcomings. Be honest and realistic with the assessment of yourself in these areas. Then, surround yourself with that which you truly love. If nature makes you feel complete, walk through and around what grows every day. Keep good, positive people around; don't allow "users" and "takers" to pull you down. Listen to your inner voice about who and what to trust. Try to avoid too much drama in your life ("a little drama will do ya ...") because peace and calm are generally prerequisites for tuning into your true feelings and also will help your health. Set small goals daily and weekly; this helps you feel like you are moving forward in your life.

I always make lists of accomplishments for the day; even the smallest, most meaningless duties that I want to complete. Getting into the habit of accomplishing is what you are trying to do here. You may not actually complete all your tasks but it sure helps towards the end result. It's all about attaining, developing, and sustaining self-discipline which acts as the steering device on your own roadmap to success. Each and every one of us defines success in a unique and individual way determined, in large part, by environmental, economic, social, and cultural factors. We all value different aspects of life yet our current society, through the media, is constantly telling us what success should look like. It is like the corporate world is trying to define success for us!

Remember, listen to your own wants and desires as to your personal success goals. We constantly hear pleas to "Save the World" but I feel the battle cry should be "Save the People." The planet will survive despite mankind. The individual, the personal self-esteem of each and every human on the globe, is at stake daily and is of the utmost importance. Collectively, "we are the world." This planet is 4 billion, 500 million years old and, guess what, it can and will last. But, we have to respect this partnership we have with nature or it is us who will pay the price. Respect of ourselves, of each other, of history and the future is the collective philosophy that can eventually eradicate the hostilities and conflicts that plague us as a people, both within ourselves and outwardly towards others.

I've given many motivational speeches in my day but one of my favorite settings was the commencement speech I gave in New York City at the Globe Institute of Technology. We were outdoors in a beautiful park-like setting in Manhattan and it is a written passage I constantly try to live by. Some quotes taken from the main text:

If you think you are beaten, you are! How true. How can you be a winner if you start with a defeatist attitude?
If you think you dare not, you don't. Never hesitate. Make a worthy decision and stick to it!
If you'd like to win but think you can't, it is almost certain that you won't. Positive attitude gives you an advantage.
If you think you will lose, you've lost. Don't set your own limits.
Success begins with a person's will. It's all in the state of mind. Mind over matter.
If you think you're outclassed, you are. Perception is key here.
You've got to think high to rise. Set goals realistically high.
You've got to be sure of yourself before you ever win a prize. Never underestimate yourself.
Life's battles won't go to the strongest or fastest man. You'll be surprised how far and fast you can push yourself and your abilities if you can totally try.

Sooner or later the one who wins is the one who thinks he can. If you gain total confidence in yourself, you are half way there before you even begin.

All in all, I was able to go on to compile a record of coaching at 29 U.S. Nationals, five Olympics, and 19 Worlds as a coach or team leader for various countries like Mexico, India, Australia, Croatia, South Korea, Canada and, of course, the good old U.S.A., along with 20 other international events. The World Championships came to us in Los Angeles, in 2009, and I was the coach and team leader for India. What an international record and what incredible experiences! This was my last World Championship as a coach and team leader and my full life student Trifun's first as a coach. What a blessing for me to share that event with him.

Decade 7: Giving Back

A Smile Starts From A Giving Heart

Give: a: to make a present of <give a doll to a child> b: to accord or yield to another <gave him her confidence> c: to commit to another as a trust or responsibility and usually for an expressed reason d: to convey to another <give them my regards> e: to present in public performance <give a concert> f: to provide by way of entertainment <give a party>
— Webster's Dictionary

Giving back ... We take so much from people and the earth. We must recycle these gifts that we are only borrowing during our lifetime. Purify and improve all gifts and pass them on to those we meet; thus, leaving our legacy. Love and share and teach all — gently, consistently, constantly. Each one of us has something to give.
— Gary Visconti

Participate In Your Own Life And The Life Of Others

Mom was always interested in the workings of politics and, on the local level, she once ran for city council. She lost but she participated and got on the ballot just to try to be part of the solution and to help make Detroit a little bit better for everyone. It was an example, to me, of determination and guts. You know, early in life we learn from example more than reading or just hearing about it.

One year, in the mid-1980s, I became spokesman for a major vitamin line in America, working with many interesting national figures on our U.S. tour. Remembering my "new" old friend Dr. John Kemeny, he once told me he spent an entire summer living with Dr. Albert Einstein back east. When John was about 23, he asked Dr. Einstein, "What is it like to be so smart?"

Dr. Einstein replied, "I am not smart, I just really try to figure things out."

Wow. How profound is that? We all can develop that concept at different levels. We all are given the choice, the challenge, and the opportunity.

Never Allow Honor To Become Extinct

In the U.S., we have a very organized group of Olympians used for lobbying, fundraising, public speaking, and inspiring young Americans to be the best they can be through sport. Honoring outstanding people and events and keeping the Olympic spirit and movement alive was one of our primary missions. Nationally, some 19,000 members participate and, in my adopted home state of California alone there are over 3,000 members. I was honored to be president of the organization for several years, from 1985 through 1988. It was a great learning experience leading this impressive group of all volunteers and gave me wonderful insight into these outstanding people and organizations such as the USOC (United States Olympic

Committee). The first three years our California Olympians office was in my home in Beverly Hills and then moved to the wonderful Amateur Athletic Headquarters which housed an incredible sports library. Contributing support and providing Olympians to over 100 events, it was a turn-key operation, and at the time a coalition of Athletes & Celebrities was formed for the Bush 1988 election.

The summer of '87 was full that year with the Presidential campaign already under way and Arnold Schwarzenegger and I heading up the Republican Coalition athletes and celebrities in the state. No less than six times were we with the Vice President at rallies and fundraisers. It was definitely a summer I will never forget. My coaching was going strong and the '88 Calgary Olympics were around the corner.

Because of our work that year on the campaign I received an invitation from the Bush team to attend the Presidential Inauguration in Washington, D.C., in January. My wife Juanita and I attended and there I met with the staff of the President's Council on Physical Fitness & Sports. There were over 200 people considered for only two newly opened spots on the Council. This is ultimately a presidential appointment and I was seriously lobbying for the position, going through the five-week governmental background investigation and a series of other interviews and "tests." On March 28th, 1988, along with my friend Arnold, I was appointed as a National Commissioner of the 12-person Council and sworn in. Little did I realize what an adventure this would become and how this honor would impact my life forever.

Influence Yourself ... And The Rest Will Follow

Arnold had a very aggressive agenda focused on the youth of America; "daily, quality physical education in the school systems" was the order of the day. His plans included visiting every governor in the Union to meet with them one-on-one and organize full-day awareness seminars in each state capital. I had the pleasure of accompanying him to over 20 of these events which he sponsored himself, funding the travel, etc. This was an incredibly valuable experience, not only to spend personal time with Arnold and each governor but to help improve the health of our young population in our school systems, one state at a time.

We had many huge projects planned including one that I created which encouraged the McDonald's Corporation to endorse a fun food fitness program. In those days, many schools around the country were using McDonald's foods in their school lunch programs. I created a "McFitness Lunch Box" for the kids with Arnold's picture on one side and the President's picture on the other. I did a presentation at the McDonald's headquarters in Chicago and, although nothing ever came from it at that time, we were able to use the McDonald's Children's Charity House for some future national youth campaigns. Funny how some ideas may be ahead of their time as it took McDonald's and others 20 years to finally realize and comply with the fact that Americans want healthier choices in their food, particularly when it comes to our children.

There were many other fun, interesting, creative, challenging events such as the "Native American Fitness Seminar" in Washington State. We had 15 tribes represented, 12 state representatives, the governor of the state and Arnold hosting the two-day event. The event was so successful that we duplicated the seminar in six other states and they all became annual events. I remember one evening on the road when Arnold and I were sitting in the hotel room telling jokes and, out of the clear blue, Arnold said, "I want to be governor."

I replied, "Of what?"

"California," he snapped.

I remember saying, "Why? You make $15 million dollars a year now and everyone loves you. As governor, you'll make $110,000 and half the state will dislike you, for sure."

His response to that was, "I just want to do it."

Well, history proved that the odds were totally against him but luck played a great hand. Gov. Gray Davis was recalled, and Arnold threw his hat into the ring and won! He made an aggressive agenda to help California recover. Of course as governor he invited me to Sacramento for many special events.

It Is Not How Much You Get But How Much You Give

We made several memorable visits to the White House during those years. I remember just before lunch break at one of the Council meetings with nine of us in attendance, Arnold received a message that simply stated: "The President would like to invite you and the Council for lunch, 12:30 in the War Room at the White House." When we arrived we were ushered into a flag-draped and paneled dining room on the main floor and we walked by a series of unique flags representing each of the wars that the United States had fought in. It was weird but interesting. As we were standing by our labeled, assigned seats at the table, the President and First Lady arrived and they were as warm and casual and sincere as I always remember them being. The President started eating first, pouring lots of tabasco sauce in his soup, and everyone else followed. I was seated next to Mrs. Bush and, being left handed, I tried not to elbow her too many times.

After lunch, the President, Arnold, and I lagged behind, slowly leaving the dining room when I very nervously asked the President, "Mr. President, how do you monitor and watch the war (this was during Desert Storm in 1991)?"

He replied, "Do you really want to know? I'll show you."

Arnold and I just stared at each other and when the President said, "Follow me," the three of us walked down a long hallway until we came to an elevator flanked by two military guards on each side. We stepped into the elevator after the President and when the doors opened on the other end of our short trip down we were looking into a room full of TV monitors and three walls lined with machines and computers and communications equipment. There were only eight to 10 people monitoring the situational War Room but they were very focused and intent and unbothered by our presence. Once in the room, the President turned to us and said, "This is where we watch everything ... on the CNN live feed." I was really surprised. Then, after just a couple of minutes, we returned upstairs, bid farewell, and went back to our Council meeting. But, it was an interlude forever etched into my memory.

Ingenuity Is Not By Accident

During this period of time, Arnold was busy shooting Terminator 2 and then Kindergarten Cop in L.A. and was extremely busy. I hung out on the set with him quite often and enjoyed every crazy, interesting moment on the sound stages, in the trailer, etc. Back in the real world and focusing on the business of getting America's youth back into shape, our most aggressive and complicated event was "The Great American Workout," hosted by the Bushes in 1991 and 1992 on the south lawn of the White House. May 1st was designated as "National Fitness Day" and we ushered it into the American way of life in a big, Hollywood way. Four months of planning and inviting celebrities, movie stars, Olympians, and pro athletes all paid off as we staged a kickoff from the steps of the Capital Building. I had a 50' x 50' ice rink constructed and filled it with Olympic Champions, NHL hockey players, and various celebrity TV performers. All the major networks covered the event with speeches given by Arnold, other fitness leaders, and comedians of note.

Later in the day, on the White House south lawn, our huge 12-stage fitness fair representing every major sport in America, all geared to both youth and senior citizen participation, was a huge success. It was attended by the Bush family, Colin Powell, Vice President Dan Quayle, and members of the House and the Senate. It was a huge logistical and security nightmare but so much fun, very successful and covered by all the major television networks. I was responsible for securing the sports talent, from Mary Lou Retton and Kristi Yamaguchi to Muhammad Ali and Jack LaLanne. The event was celebrated in all 50 states at each state capital. That evening, Sargent Shriver and Eunice Kennedy Shriver (Maria's parents) hosted a fabulous party at their home in Virginia. What fun we had with Milton Berle and the like "roasting" each other. The talent and celebrity in that group was truly historical ... and hysterical.

So many fun experiences with Arnold. He loves big vehicles, tanks, etc. Early in about 1990 he took three of us to the Hummer plant in Indiana with Hiro Yamagata as our "fun" photographer. Of course we received VIP treatment and a fun, crazy, off-road, rough terrain test drive of two of these military-only machines. Well, I drove one with a coach in the shotgun seat, and Arnold was driving behind me, close to my tail throughout the 30-minute (impossible) drive. Up and down cliffs, through rivers, swamps and 45 degree angular roads and paths, I was sweating it.

When I was coming out of the river on a huge bank and he was on my tail — like only four feet back — all I could think of was rocking backward into him. The coach said, "Inflate the tires now and you'll get more traction," and it worked. Saved, but how crazy!

Back at the plant, Arnold ordered a Humvee and the company was off and running to conform it to a street-worthy legal vehicle. Arnold took delivery 10 months later and the popular Humvee was born.

We All Come, We All Go; It's What We Leave Behind

Me and Arnold Schwarzenegger on the ice at the White House.

Visiting with Milton Berle.

ARNOLD SCHWARZENEGGER

October 11, 1999

Mr. Gary C. Visconti
1314 Pacific Avenue
Venice Beach, CA 90291

Dear Gary:

Thanks so much for the unique and wonderful birthday present. As you know, I enjoy art very much, and I am especially honored to have a piece painted just for me!

The use of color and character in the painting itself is very interesting, and I am already searching for the perfect place to hang up this new addition to my art collection.

It is always great to hear from you, and I hope we can see each other soon. This birthday gift is a very special one, and I thank you again for your generosity.

With my best,

Arnold Schwarzenegger

AS/bae

When are you coming to one of our cigar nights? I hope to see you soon 😊

A thank you letter from Arnold.

At my Olympian office in the Amateur Athletic Foundation in Los
Angeles

Me and President George H.W. Bush!

Following Page:

Top: Giving testimony in Washington D.C., for the Fitness
Council.

Bottom: Me and Jack LaLanne promoting fitness.

THE WHITE HOUSE

WASHINGTON

May 22, 1990

Dear Gary:

Just a note of thanks for your participation in the Great American Workout. This event was a success because you volunteered your time to help demonstrate some of the fun and exciting ways people of all ages can become physically fit. Your continuing efforts to spread the word about the benefits of exercise will help ensure Americans a bright and healthy future.

Barbara joins me in sending thanks and best wishes.

Sincerely,

George Bush

The Honorable Gary Visconti
Suite 3
273 Spalding Drive
Beverly Hills, California 90212

A letter from President George H.W. Bush!

With my sister and Mohammad Ali.

Me, Julia and Colin Powell.

Working with Arnold!

We served the President until his last week in office when we were invited to the Oval Office for a goodbye visit and photo opportunity. It was really a sad time for the President because he seemed so in shock about leaving office or, at least, that is how I read him that day. Ten months earlier he had been riding high in the polls with his Desert Storm victory but I think his domestic policy was not strong and then, also, people forget very quickly about his wonderful international diplomacy that marked his career. That week I mentioned to Arnold in his plane on our return trip to L.A. that I wanted to keep working on fitness programs. He advised me to put together my own Foundation for Fitness. I loved the idea and soon formed the United Fitness Foundation in early 1993. Based in Los Angeles, we promoted local fitness fairs and had various Olympians give motivational speeches at schools in Southern California. The Foundation did a lot of good and continued with its mission until 1998.

It Is Not "Save the Planet," It's Save The Reason For Being On The Planet

During these busy years I continued hot and heavy with coaching and being director at the local skating rink. One of my prized students of 13 years was Trifun Zivanovic. When the 1999 skating season got under way, Trifun was 23 years of age (my Olympic age) and I had him primed to make the World Team. In January of that year, he had an outstanding performance at Nationals and won the Silver Medal, placing him on the World Team where he had a great showing in Finland.

In Boston in 2001, proudly coaching Trifun toward another silver or possibly gold medal at the U.S. National Championships, I was equally excited because that week during the closing ceremonies in the Boston Stadium, I, with my great colleague John Nicks, were to be inducted into the U.S. Figure Skating Hall of Fame. Imagine, some 26 years after he first took me under his wing and mentored me toward international coaching ... a real honor. That was one of the hardest and most gratifying speeches I have ever given in front of my peers, champions and fans alike, from the past 50 years. It was truly a special moment in my life.

As it turned out, Trif skated flawlessly, but lost his birth on the World Team because that year America qualified only two men to compete at Worlds, which was a blow to us. But, as always, he stood tall and gracious. It was a temporary blow but continued to build the resiliency that Trifun would become known for. His mom ran his career and she was a very strong-willed woman. When she became wheelchair bound with MS it seemed to only add to her determination to push and promote her son. Always working the angles in her effort to advance his career, she pulled Trifun away from me three times as his primary coach, always thinking that maybe somebody else could offer her son a golden ticket to the promise land of skating. Each time I was disappointed because I had always given him my all and brought him so close to elite stature and, each time, the Zivanovics would come back home to me, realizing indeed that we had something special together.

Patience Is Learned... But Not Without Practice

I helped sponsor Trifun through the years and, in the end, he became National Champion and a five-time competitor at World's for his father's native country of Serbia/Montenegro. Trifun competed at the 2006 Olympics in Italy and our last competition together was at the World Championships in Japan in 2007. I was, and am, so proud of Trifun. What a full career he had; 14 International Championships, 10 Nationals, the Olympics — outstanding! We topped it all off by both being official coaches at the 2009 World Championships in Los Angeles representing two different countries — Trifun his Serbia and myself, India. It would be his first World coaching experience and my last.

Being at the Olympic Games several times I was able to relive my own special experience from 1968. Only now some 20 or 30 years older and because I was Team Leader for a particular country, I lived in the Athletes Village while my coach colleagues had to stay some five miles away in the Coaches Village. I usually received many envious remarks about that. It did give me an opportunity to bond with and enjoy the entire "athlete experience" again from a whole new mature viewpoint. Boy, these competitors are treated like hot house tomatoes ... talk about royal treatment! Good for them as they deserve every advantage.

Dreams Are For Those Who Strive

During one of the very busiest times of my coaching career when the rink was going well and I had plenty of students and programs to promote in 2004, a funny thing happened in my professional career as I was "bit" by the "Glamour Ice Bug" as I like to refer to it. One of my very good, long-time skating friends, Bonnie Jo Parker, approached me about creating a new professional ice review. I remember her sales pitch to me as, "Gary, I have the money and you have all the contacts and the name in skating, so what do you think?" After some thought I agreed and so was born "Legends on Ice." The mission statement was to bring back the glamour and spectacle of the classic ice reviews such as "The Hollywood Ice Review," "The Ice Follies," and "The Ice Capades," all huge traveling ice reviews with over 90 performers, various acts, and featured stars. These ice reviews toured North America for nine months each year and were very successful from the 1940s through 1998.

As they faded out due to high salaries, exorbitant arena rental fees, transportation costs, etc., the "Champions on Ice" tour took over. The concept for that format was to feature only top World and Olympic talent with no fluff, no props, and no productions, just a recital type review appearing for one night only in 20 major cities. Tommy Collins was the fantastic promoter and creator and kept the whole event very skater and fan friendly. For years it was successful but Bonnie and I felt there was a market for an ice spectacular if it was put together correctly and had a real theme, glitz, glamour, and talent.

If You're Not Shaken, You're Not Moving.

It was my job to pull together just the right combination of experienced, professional people to make it all work, and I did. Our crew and creators were the best. Our choreographer, Bob Turk (30-plus years of experience with Ice Capades and stage shows), and our costume shops, music director and crew where all top notch and first rate. Only Bonnie and I were the "newbies" in this realm of producing skating, and totally responsible for its success or failure. We designed a two-hour and 20-minute production with a 20-minute intermission. We featured 12 soloist and six major production numbers with 12 female and eight male line dancers. The whole show was dedicated to skating legends yet the look was kept contemporary. We only had four weeks of full rehearsal to put it on ice and teach the very talented line skaters. Each one of the featured ice stars had their own solos and were responsible for their own music and costumes.

Scheduled to open in the Long Beach, California, arena on November 4th, we only had 48 hours to test the entire show's mechanics and rehearse the final run-through. All went well but it was extremely stressful to pull everyone together in such a short period of time. Dorothy Hamill and Elvis Stojko were fantastic to work with and great crowd pleasers. Other famous performers included Nicole Bobek, Trifun, Tai Babilonia and Randy Gardner, Rudy Galindo, Ken Shelley and JoJo Starbuck, Dan Hollender, and various novelty acts.

In the blackout sitting on a wooden stool the announcer was introducing "The U.S., North American, and World Professional Champion, Ladies and Gentleman ... Mr. Gary Visconti." Sitting there it felt like 10 minutes, and had the music not started and spotlights not picked me up, I think I would have fainted. What the hell am I doing? Performing on ice after some 35 years of NOT skating, I was nuts and in front of 9,000 people.

This was me in Long Beach Arena, where I had made my Senior debut at the U.S. National in 1963, 42 years ago! I am now co-executive producer of "Legends on Ice." I guess a legend skating to a legend ... Mr. Frank Sinatra's "My Way" played ... a cameo appearance of my own. I am really nuts. Sixty years old and nuts.

Everyone was housed at the Hilton Hotel in Long Beach for the week and the concept of all these fabulous people together in one show with Dick Button as the master of ceremonies was truly historic. Our after-show party was held on the Queen Mary ship in Long Beach Harbor. We hosted 300 "black-tie" guests, an orchestra and a full dinner, and presented Dick Button with the "Lifetime Achievement Award."

The Rest Of The Story ...

The show had been put together over a four-month period and all the funding was from Bonnie Joe's family and in-laws. I knew nothing of the funding or the expenses or the forms of payment made and I was never consulted on that part of the show. My contract as co-executive producer with Bonnie's Gala Entertainment Co. called for no salary, just a generous percentage of the company's profit. Bonnie and I worked tirelessly and endlessly together to produce the best product on ice we could conceive of, and it worked. Our opening in Long Beach was a tremendous success, with many special people in the audience including the booking president for Caesar's Palace, Las Vegas. Caesar's wanted our show! We flew to Las Vegas two weeks later and worked out a deal in which we would supply a large ice rink outside in front of the hotel so that in the months of November, December, and January we could have daily ice skating on their property; a huge draw for the hotel. The term was "four-walled the event," which meant that we would provide everything and the hotel/casino would provide rooms and food for the entire cast and crew. When showtime came around the weather was not in our favor and as I looked out over the slushy ice and the sparsely scattered audiences, my heart began to melt ... and break.

I was working 20 hours a day trying to hold the performances together while Bonnie was dealing with overrun expenses for practically every phase of the operation, including the huge payroll it took to put on a featured 70-minute nightly show. The reviews were good but, in the end, the money was just not there. It was a bitter experience having invested thousands and thousands of unpaid "volunteer" hours — plus blood, sweat, and tears — into a project that we really believed in and one that had started off so well, with so much promise. Personally, I had jeopardized my coaching career and had no income for many months. Financially it was a real flop, but still a fantastic show and learning experience.

No Battles End Without Scars ... Keep The Will To Win, The Freedom
To Fail

I really believe that one reason why we don't give back as much as we could or should or "really want to but can't" is because we feel injured by life, harmed by unjust events, ripped off ourselves by crueler fates. We are hurting inside and, therefore, focused on "me," not the "we" or "us" or "them." To get outside of ourselves and into the shoes of someone else is not only healing but rewarding, and we grow from it.

One season Sharon Jimenez, my dear friend and P.R. woman, entered some of my paintings into the National Olympian's art competition. Oh no, do I compete again? With my consent we sent two pieces of work, and I won first place nationally. Then 17 countries exhibited in Italy, and my work won first place there also, and went on a world tour of 12 countries. What a great compliment to my efforts and now five years later I have exhibited many times and have started selling some of my pieces. It's fun and rewarding ... a new challenge and learning ground ... so keep ready for anything.

Your personal outlook on life is, I believe, the single most influential ingredient in living a "successful" life. It is how you look at any given situation that can make or break it — and you. I feel we usually sabotage ourselves throughout our lives, unintentionally, in one way or another. Many times we fear we will fail. Other times we feel that we are unworthy of success or feel that we won't be able to hold onto it and keep to that high standard once we achieve it. We definitely are our own worst enemy all too often; don't give into this!

It must have been about 2007 when Sharon and I put together a television series concept show for elite figure skaters the world never got to see perform nationally, called "Ice Warriors." Yes, a reality show ... competitive, creative, living together, and all the drama and heartache that goes along with it. Coaches, choreographers, challenges and injuries, both physical and mental. At the 10-week climax of the show, champions would receive a prize that would be a featured solo with the traveling 20-city tour of "Stars on Ice," a company of strictly World and Olympic ice champions of which these winners would not be. We had several high-level meetings and all went fantastic. In the end, our runner (the person who was to take our concept to a network) tried to control the entire venture and after a long inner struggle, and over our lack of experience in this area, Sharon and I let it die. I guess we opened the door for others now!

To Discover Yourself Is The Real Treasure

Do you want to know the best way to get out of your own way? Gratitude, pure and simple. Blessings come to us in so many different forms. Look around your immediate life — they are everywhere! And if you'll take the time daily to recognize them and recognize others, you'll be well on your way towards being the most successful you that you can be.

Remember, success is perceived by you but, no matter your definition, giving of yourself to others is the crowning jewel of a life well lived. We are never truly whole and complete if we are not, ultimately, filling up someone else's life with the riches of our own. We plan, we compete for our dreams and we fulfill our destiny to various degrees. We love along the way, hopefully sharing from our heart and teaching from our life experience, but let us always be giving back in a way that makes a real difference in someone's life and in the lives of all we come across ... leaving this world, this environment, and all its inhabitants better off than when we found it.

The Integrity Of Men Is Only Limited By Desire Of Giving And Honesty

Afterword

Just like anyone else — everyone else, I suspect — good advice has been hard to come by and even harder to live by. In some respects, it has taken me a lifetime to learn and to understand myself, let alone the world and others around me. I'm still learning every day, a student of the universe and all it has to teach. My only one true regret in life is that I do not have another 70 years on this Earth to live, to give, to love, to share and learn.

As I have stumbled though the past years of my life — experiences and people, good and bad — have taught me humans are capable of anything. We are multifaceted creatures driven by curiosity, love, desire and greed. History has proven this as we have not learned, only continually repeating its failures. Throughout my life I have tried to initiate a "better me" by writing small goals. These have eventually become some 700 short sayings or "Garyisms." Some for self, some for humanity, some as unreachable concepts, but all meant for better understanding of self, the world we wish to live in, and others. It has never been my intention to "preach" or reprimand, or even guide, only encourage through the reincarnation of heritage, honor, and values set by history's conceptual treasures: Love, understanding, and respect of others. Take from these treasures what you can to learn about self, value life, our world, and grow and improve daily so you may be armed to bring your dream to reality on the road to fulfill your destiny.

Engage And Expand ... Life

One thing I can say is that I really don't look back in life; I'm always looking ahead to what is left undone and to what I still want to accomplish. I figure life is like stepping across stones in a river — you had better concentrate on the rock you are on and focus on the next one or else you will slip and fall back.

What You Gain When You Lose Is Immeasurable

I have fallen down thousands of times and I have definitely learned (the hard way) that the important thing is not the falling, but the getting up and trying again, and again, and again. In fact, I have never learned anything significant about myself when I won a championship, but everything I needed to know about myself when I lost.

Many people don't even try for fear of failure or fear of disappointing others when what they should fear is letting themselves down. I remember "shedding" perfection at age 18 and, you know what, I became a very good skater very quickly after that. Perfect, no. Persistent, yes!

To me, self-motivation is plugging into your own inner strength, desire, and resources. External motivation is distracting; internal motivation is empowering. So, participate in your own life, with passion for yourself and others.

Remember, laughter really is the "good drug" and love the highest high. The best advice I can give you: Life can be fatal ... so, fun it!

I love you. I really do. And I wish for you all the success that you can dream of and imagine!

— *Gary Visconti*

P.S. I truly hope that I have not offended anyone. My stories, times, dates and events are meant to share for growth and understanding. All has been written to the best of my memory to allow you to experience the journey of my most blessed life.

The "Roasting" of Gary Visconti

" ... with a little help from my friends"

"Barbara and I would like to extend our heartfelt thanks for all your efforts on our behalf. Your superb contribution to the President's Council on Physical Fitness and Sports these years have made America a 'fitter nation'."
— President George H.W. Bush

"So 'Low Forehead,' you proved to be my funny, friendly, fancy, figure-skating friend from the fifties; again! Thanks for helping make America a fitter and healthier nation."
— Arnold Schwarzenegger

"Twenty years ago I met with Gary Visconti at his place of business and I asked him to teach me how to skate so that I could play hockey. He asked me how old I was. (I didn't look young.) I said I was 65 and he said, 'why would I waste my time teaching a guy to skate who isn't going to be around a long time?' He taught me and I'm still here!"
— Frank Gehry

"Gary Visconti was the innovator of bringing style, form, and athletic grace to modernizing figure skating."
— Vera Wang

"Gary and I experienced through the sport of figure skating a discovery about ourselves that we were not aware of in our teenage years. We were not just competing. Win or lose, we were learning life lessons that would help us the rest of our lives!"

— Peggy Fleming Jenkins

"Gary Visconti is everything I can't stand. He's a great looking guy that never gets older. Everyone who knows him, loves him. And to be one of the greatest skaters the U.S. has ever produced ... you get the idea. But that's also why I respect, admire, and love the guy. There aren't enough Gary Viscontis in the world. I wish there were more."

— Scott Hamilton

"Some people can be accused of skating through life, but in Gary Visconti's case, that would be a great compliment. I am so fortunate to have worked with Gary for a number of years, and enjoyed being coached by the very best there is!"

— Jerry Bruckheimer

Gary's Celebrity Impressions

Dorothy Hamill: A real athletic presence; strong, a true sports hero. Dealt with a lot of insecurity early in life and has become a solid and giving woman. Six years with her after winning the Olympics gave me a great perspective on confidence building and understanding how different elite athletes tick. Unpredictable, and yet so lovable and resilient.

Gov. Arnold Schwarzenegger: Knowing him some 25 years, I have been with him in many roles. He is serious and funny, always looking for a new challenge and a mark to leave along the way. Bringing great people together to achieve great roles, with his great ideas. And when you fail ... you are a low forehead! A professional kidder and joker!

President George H.W. Bush: After meeting several presidents, President Bush and his wife Barbara were the most comfortable and down to earth. My respect for his vast international diplomacy and all-encompassing wisdom grew with each visit. Stronger on an international scale, weaker on domestic challenges, a truly modern American cornerstone.

Scott Hamilton: Dealt a bad hand physically at birth, sport made him physically and mentally complete. Humble and true to himself, never complaining, always listening ... a dream student with an unsurpassed work ethic.

Frank Gehry: Using line, harmony, efficiency and functionality — usability — to make the world look and function better. Monuments to his genius stand worldwide.

Maria Shriver: Strong of character and a reverence for values; a journalist's dream. A woman of future vision who knows how to attract great people to help accomplish her goals for humanity. Giving of herself and striving for a better world.

Jerry Bruckheimer: Always thinking, mentally recording what he sees and hears and taking it 100 steps beyond to become something special for all to enjoy on the screen; a true visionary. Very serious, on guard a real analyzer of life and all it brings.

Wilt Chamberlain: His love of life and self-confidence as a man and sports star kept him three notches above the rest. A great host, he appreciated life to its fullest and lived it.

Luc Robitaille: Working with him in the early years of his professional career, his rough technique but great skill put him in the right place at the right time to take the team to victory. A true team player. Always ready for a joke or a funny moment; flexible but committed.

Outtake Stories

From 1985 to 1988, Juanita and I initiated "celeb skate night" at the Culver Arena, at every Thursday late skate. All told there were about 30 of us, and at least five to 10 were in town each Thursday night. Dean and Squint, Billie Hench, Desi Arnaz, Lynn Holly Johnson, Arnold, staff from his office, some NHL hockey players, Hiro Yamagata, plus Linda Pearl and various others. We had a blast!

* * *

After our huge ice skating rally at the steps of the Capital Building in Washington D.C. with Kristi Yamaguchi and Scott Hamilton on ice — that television segment hosted by Faith Daniels and attended by over 60 congressional members — we got ready for television interviews all promoting "National Fitness Day" on May 1st nationwide. It was 1991 and this was the Great American Workout! We were on the south lawn of the White House two hours later, hosted by President and Mrs. Bush, with some 85 celebrities and athletes in attendance representing 16 different fitness, fun, and health sports. Maria's parents, Eunice and Sargent Shriver, hosted a gala party at their home in Virginia that evening. Oh my God, it was so fabulous! Milton Berle, Jack LaLanne, Colin Powell, Flo Joe, Mary Lou Retton, Peter Vidmar, Mohammad Ali, and of course Arnold; all of us partied and socialized till late. I remember when we arrived, boxer Sugar Ray Leonard was there when we entered the front reception. He turned to Juanita and I and said, "My dog could do his business for a year on these grounds and no one would ever find it." We hit it off just fine with that statement.

* * *

214

Wilt Chamberlain was too cool, and at seven feet two and half inches tall, he lived up the road from us in Bel Air on Mulholland and was a huge fan of skating. Frequenting each others' homes, I remembered it was his birthday one year so I bought ice skates for him, specially sized at 14-1/2 D. We had them delivered to his home with 20 helium balloons. When they arrived, the housekeeper accepting the delivery, and he came home very late that evening. His was a very dark and quiet house; he saw shadows in the front entryway, something moving very strangely. He had come in the garage, so he got his gun and came to the front entry, yelled and fired a shot into the dark. Turning on the light, he was puzzled and couldn't believe his eyes ... and then laughed for three days. Boy, I'll never live that one down.

* * *

To celebrate Dorothy Hamill's 21st birthday we had a huge celebrity filled "Ice Broom Ball" at the chalet. In attendance were some fun people, like singer Kenny Rogers, who unfortunately broke Juanita's wrist with his overactive broom while competing on the ice in his tennis shoes during our mock hockey match. Desi Arnaz Jr. and Gina Martin, and Dean of course, who had just finished a film with Ali McGraw. Also Andy Gibb (The Bee Gees), actress Linda Pearl, Lynn Holly Johnson, David Cassidy, Wilt Chamberlain, and many more. Juanita and I had so much fun putting it all together for her, and surprised her by getting her to the ice arena for a late practice. She came very reluctantly. Surprise! Boy, we got her!

* * *

Dean's younger sister Gina took to the ice and after Juanita had been coaching her for 10 months, really wanted to get away on her own and try out for a chorus spot in the world famous Ice Capades. Well, she made the cut and was so elated to travel for one season with the show on her own.

* * *

I remember one night Dorothy and Juanita took three hours to get ready for a special party at her manager's home, Jerry Weintraub. They drove to the party ... no valet, no other cars around, the grounds of the home seemed empty. They thought they were too early. Well, they knocked on the door, Jerry answered, and guess what? It was the wrong day! The party was the next night. Embarrassing! We all laughed for days. The next night all went well with the event and Governor Jerry Brown, Linda Ronstadt and Rev. Jesse Jackson kidded them all evening.

* * *

As a special birthday present for Dorothy, for her 24th birthday in 1981, Dean and Juanita filmed a special 18-minute crazy fun ice film that I directed, produced, and wrote. We called it "Ice Sickies," and it starred one of our national Senior skaters, Ken Newfield. She loved the entire thing and Dean worked at least 50 hours on the ice to learn some special moves for this spoof film. He was truly great, a trooper and a fine athlete.

* * *

Remembering some fun, crazy celebrity friends and situations ... In the early 1980s our daughter Michele went to school with little Courtney Wagner, Robert Wagner and Natalie Wood's child. The girls became good friends and had sleepovers at both of our homes. I remember one Halloween all the kids went trick or treating in our Beverly Hills community. Robert drove and Natalie rode shotgun. We all sat in back of the station wagon and the girls went to so many fun homes; friends such as Fred Astaire and so many more. Real good fun! Later that week Natalie dropped Courtney off for a sleepover and fell in love with our antique burrowed wood piano from England, and really wanted to buy it. But Juanita had a special place in her heart for it and would not sell it — I bought it for our fifth wedding anniversary — even though she offered 10 times what I paid for it. Robert was the star of the very popular and long-running television series Hart to Hart and we were frequently on the set. He was always a true gentleman and friend. He took us to the set of M.A.S.H. and The Love Boat where Alan Alda and all the actors welcomed us. Such fun professional people, and always a positive experience.

* * *

When I was Champion in 1965, Scotty Allen and Peter Meyers — a bad boy skater — and I were all starring in a summer festival show. I remember that it was the big Labor Day Weekend show where I had won my first title in Lake Placid. We practiced in the afternoon and then took a break, coming back to skate in the evening. At 4 p.m. I left my skates in the dressing room and then came back a few hours later to skate as the star of the greatly anticipated yearly Ice Extravaganza. My skates felt really funny as I made my way out to take my start position. I thought maybe some dirt was on my blades. I started my program ... and fell. I got up, did a back crossover, and fell. I got up, did a three turn, and fell. I didn't know what to do so I waved apologetically to the audience and pointed down to my skates and shrugged my shoulders, and then made my way off the ice. Turns out, during that afternoon break someone had taken the edges off my blades! Hmm ... very interesting! Who could that have been? Maybe the Lake Placid Village "bad boy" with a jealous vendetta? We will probably never know, for Peter has gone way before his time.

* * *

Having the unique opportunity of being surrounded by L.A. and all it offers, a call came into my office at the ice arena and the voice at the other end said, "I represent a person that would like to employ you as his ice hockey development instructor. He would like to rent the entire arena privately for these workouts."

I said, "No, really, there is no time available for that and it truly is not necessary. I've coached very famous people on late morning ice, with limited elite skaters on the ice ... no one really pays attention to who's who. High profile or not, we train here."

So two days later a kind of shy, quiet guy walks in and introduces himself. "Hi, I'm Mike Myers, nice to meet you."

He was cool, and not a bad skater at all, and he really improved. Never did see any of his fun movies.

* * *

Fun times when in walk two people, one guy real friendly, who sticks out his hand and says, "I've heard you are one of the best coaches. I used to play hockey in Canada. Can you work with me? I'm Jim Carrey."

"Oh, well I'll see if I can help you improve your skills. Got five years?"

He laughed and said, "It's a pleasure to meet an Olympian. So you'll take me on?"

"Okay," I said. "Let's try."

He was great and what fun, too. We started that day. A true gentleman and quite a nice skater ... now!

In my early years of ice skating and throughout my career our competitive skating routine music was on vinyl records, cut from reel-to-reel tape machines which Mr. Don liked to edit by hand at home. He would cut the actual tape with a razor blade and then splice the two ends together. It could take six hours. Then we would take our cut, edited versions of some classical music over to the recording studio and sit there and watch them press the actual 78 rpm record as per our exact requests. We did this all in Detroit in the three-story house in downtown called Motown Records. I still remember climbing the back stairs (all three stories) up to the studio. One time I was about 17 years old, and coming down those stairs slowly were three people. Mr. Don said, "Gary, stop. Watch out, that kid is blind." It was Stevie Wonder! I just stared ... who would have thought; and history would note such a legendary musician and master of obstacles, a true hero of the entertainment world.

* * *

On one of my last visits to the White House I remember mentioning to President Bush, "Mr. President, having been with you so many times over the past four years I do not have a photo of us together."

As we were walking out of the luncheon he answered, "Well, Gary, let's do that now." So the President scurried into the hall and yelled, "Frank! Frank, I need you!" Frank was the official White House photographer. "I can't find him," said the President.

I was a little embarrassed and said, "Oh, it's okay, we can do it next time."

Such a down-to-earth and easy-going man; he made us all feel so comfortable each visit.

* * *

Talk about passion for ice hockey and skating. Jerry Bruckheimer one morning brings to me his detailed plans for a full ice rink, "barn style," for his huge horse ranch in Kentucky. "Gary, you spent almost 50 years daily in an ice arena. How can I improve this concept?" We had fun going over many various details. The result is truly cool. He and his NHL hockey friends use it often.

* * *

Frank Gehry got his hand in designing the entire training facility ice arena for the Mighty Ducks team in Anaheim, California. There was a large curved roof of wood, of course, covering both arenas; truly airy and open, a real skaters' paradise.

* * *

Having the pleasure of coaching and helping so many celebrities, no one was more challenging than Arnold. I wish I could say he was a dream to coach. It was more like "Godzilla meets the ballet." He, I am sure, does better in the water, not walking on top of it. But I am sure he thinks he walks on it anyway. He is always up for a huge personal challenge.

* * *

Ice show pranks: In Mexico City, at one of our last performances of the season for Holiday on Ice, one of the ugly sisters (Mike Course), during the very formal 25-minute production of "Cinderella," pre-set a small explosive inside the glass slipper. Yes, you got it. When Prince Charming (Ray Balmer) found it on the castle step and held it up to admire, Mike set it off. Crazy! Ray threw it down in dismay ... but the show must go on! Mike Course later received a hefty fine.

* * *

While on tour in Europe with the Holiday on Ice tour, Christmas was in Prague, Czechoslovakia, and kind of lonely. I did receive some gifts and many cards from home. One special gift kept following me around Europe and in April, that Christmas gift finally caught up to me in Paris. Yes, it was a fruitcake. Yum.

* * *

During our first World Tour in 1966 we spent about 16 days in the U.S.S.R. They were good to us; we received per-diem spending money in rubles each day. I never spent much of it and when it came time to leave I had a few hundred which I would not take out of the country. So for Mom I bought a mink stole, with Mr. Don's financial help. She cherished it for 15 years until she passed.

* * *

It's around the summer of 1968 and Vlad came to North American with the Soviet U.S.S.R. Wrestling Team as a guard. We had kept in correspondence for two years now. They came to Toledo, Ohio, about 45 miles from Detroit. Of course we met up there and Mr. Don and I viewed some great competitive matches, U.S. versus U.S.S.R.

Afterward, Nikoli Snetkov and Vlad wanted to see an American burlesque show. Guess they heard Toledo was the place, so we went. Oh my God, trashy and an eye-opener for me, even at 23. Enough about the Cold War ... that was HOT!

* * *

After a very long 19-hour day of three states, three governors, and three fitness seminars, Arnold and I are flying home at 10 p.m. Both of us drained, relaxed and half asleep, facing each other on his jet, at the table looking out the window at the magnificently lit city beneath us. I said, "Look at all those lights."

He said, "Just think of all the people making love right now."

I calmly said, "Yeah, and you'll be with Maria partaking real soon and I'll be thinking about you."

He very quietly said, "And I won't be thinking about you!"

* * *

Remembering one summer in 1978 or so, Dorothy and Juanita were on the road with Ice Capades and they were coming home tomorrow. I thought to wash Dorothy's Mercedes 380 SL. It was new, but dirty. I usually checked out her house twice a week while they were gone as well. I cleaned the inside of the car, trashing some Kleenex and water bottles. They came home and the next day Squint called me and asked, "Did you clean my car? And where is the Kleenex that was in the ashtray?"

I told her I trashed it. "Oh, no! Inside were my two-carat diamond earrings!"

Well, I panicked and flew over to her house and it was trash day! I found the discarded wad of Kleenex after one hour of garbage searching. Wow! Saved.

* * *

At Bell Isle, a huge state park reserve and year-round attraction for Detroit, it must have been the winter of 1955. The park is in the middle of the Detroit River. Dad took my eight-year-old sister Debby and I ice skating on the natural ice. Well, as adventurous kids would, we went too far from Dad and toward the middle of the huge river. The ice gave way and Debby disappeared. I froze. Dad yelled, "Don't move, son! I'll get Debby!" I saw her except she was at my feet, under the ice, staring up at me. It was like the earth stood still. Dad did somehow retrieve her and that terrible few moments could have cured me from ever wanting to ice skate again. But somehow destiny was not interrupted.

* * *

At the 1965 U.S. Nationals, last men's practice before the one freestyle competition that night, I was in first place in the preliminaries (which counted for 60 percent) and I was feeling the pressure. Mr. Don was not pleased and he was standing on the television camera platform at my eye level from the ice. I wasn't completing my triple jump. As I was standing there listening to his "correction" my hand was on the platform. To make sure I heard the message he stepped very firmly on my fingers and said, smiling, "If you don't execute this next triple I'll crush your hand." So, yeah, with 500 people watching of course I did it just fine and the practice time was over, thank God!

* * *

Coming home from the Cup of Russia in the early 2000s with Trifun we got totally detained at customs upon arrival back into the U.S. The dogs sniffed us out of like 300 passengers. Talk about a thorough search ... turning pages in our magazines and all! After 1.5 hours of intense searching they gave up. I requested the official completely re-pack all of our bags (as was customary), and she was upset that I knew the procedure. Running and almost missing our two-hour connection, I was questioning Trifun all the way. After we were home for two days he called me and said, "Gary, I was wearing my black leather jacket home from Russia and I wore the same jacket 15 days earlier here in L.A. at a party the night before we left and the kids were smoking pot. But really, I didn't and I don't!"

Well, mystery solved. I could have killed him. So for two years I must have had a red flag on my name at customs because every time I entered the U.S. it was like the third degree.

* * *

Davos, Switzerland, at the 1966 Worlds and Mom and I were walking the town after practice. I stopped at a store window and saw the coolest black leather-like skate bag. Love at first sight! We went in and wow it was expensive — over $25.00 U.S. I was disappointed. She said, "If you medal here, it's yours."

I skated my heart out for that bag and it was on the plane going home with me. I still have and use it today.

* * *

I was excited about closing our European tour in April after a six-week run in Paris. The two-and-a-half-month vacation break back in the U.S.A. was truly welcomed. August of 1970 found me rehearsing the new show in Knoxville, Tennessee. Our opening in September at Madison Square Garden was to be fantastic. I had new custom clothes made while in Europe and had my entire belongings in my huge oversized wardrobe trunk. The show's responsibility was to transport these during the tour. Well, the train car hauling all our trunks caught fire while on route to New York City and we all lost everything. To top it all off, only the trunk itself was insured, and not the contents. We each received $327.00 for our loss.

Gary is ...

A son

A brother

An uncle

A godfather

A skater

An artist

A college student

A professional picture framer

A State Champion

A U.S. Champion

A North American Champion

An Olympian

A World Professional Champion

An international athlete

An ice show performer

A television commentator

A big-screen ice movie choreographer

A national coach

A world coach

An Olympic coach

A husband

A father

A grandfather

A U.S. Presidential Appointee

A major ice review producer

A painter

Winner, U.S. Olympian's Art Festival

Past president of the California Olympian's Association

Owner of Pro Skates, Inc.

Head Coach and Figure Skating Director, Culver City Ice Arena

A member of the U.S. Figure Skating Hall of Fame

Co-founder and Board Member of the Bring Hollywood Home
Foundation

A motivational speaker

Student of the universe

... And a new author

Gary has ...

Served on 20 committees

Served on five foundations

Been a member of seven associations

Been president of six organizations

Been CEO of two foundations

Had one presidential appointment

Met 10 heads of state

Traveled to 42 states, 29 countries, and five continents

Given over 3,200 live performances

Had over 300 TV appearances

Been a live on-air commentator three times

Worked on five big screen movies

Been on 10 TV shows, and seven live shows

Produced "Legends on Ice" at Caesar's Palace, Las Vegas, and
    Tropicana Casino, Atlantic City, New Jersey

Appeared in over 80 national publications and on the cover of
    numerous national and international magazines

Worked on two presidential campaigns

Been co-founder of the Bring Hollywood Home Foundation 501c4

Been inducted into the Figure Skating Hall of Fame, Colorado Springs,
    Colorado

Personally skated the equivalent to 1.5 times around the earth ... some
    36,000 miles

Fallen down over 200,000 times on the ice, at least

God, I have a fear of ...

Losing my motivational strength

Losing my health

Losing my financial independence

Offending special people

Not advancing in life

Trying something new I can't finish

Losing my opportunity to achieve something new

Losing my looks

Not knowing you, God

Falling short of my own expectations and those of others

Losing my ability to influence others in a positive way

Lord, universe, please remove these fears. I pray only for knowledge and understanding, and for You to instill faith so I may carry out Your will and my destiny.

Things I hate ...

War

Swimming in the ocean

Height

Extreme heat

Being trapped in an elevator

Loud, loud, people

Being reprimanded

Getting caught in a little white lie

Wasting time

Traffic, stopped on a freeway

People acting entitled to do whatever they want

Body piercing

People not respecting others

Mis-matched clothes

Looking not current

Messy rooms

Overpriced — anything!

Humanity suffering

Animals neglected

People not in perspective

Very over-indulging parents

Close-minded people

Abusing anything

Ignoring tradition

Losing someone's trust

Becoming too confident

Being passive

What I believe…

I believe our destiny is set at birth, but the path is directed by us

There is other intelligent life in the universe

We are all connected through a universal life force

We are responsible for ourselves

There are good and evil forces in the world, competing

We are God-like in all aspects

We make our own heaven or hell

We must help each other find internal peace

We should leave a strong legacy behind

We cannot waste life's precious moments

No one is a sinner

You are what you think you are

Not all people are meant to be parents

The first five years of life sets your mind and values

We learn from parental example

We all have too much … too many things

We don't take time to praise nature, and must, always

Keep your heart for yourself

Everyone must travel the globe

The world is really one

We are what we eat and how we think

Man will soon become extinct, through greed

It's okay to be scared, but do it!

We can control our minds and thoughts

We must manage our own health, be responsible

We should stay involved in life, with a drive and a purpose

We should listen to people carefully

You shouldn't do too much, but what you do, do it right!

We should keep learning ... but keep advice to ourselves

Accomplishments

- Figure Skating Hall of Fame Member
- Five-time U.S. World Team Member
- U.S. Olympic Figure Skating Team Member
- 1965-1967 North American Men's Champion
- 1965-1967 U.S. Men's Champion
- 1964 Junior Men's World Figure Skating Champion, Garmisch, Germany
- 1969 World Professional Champion, London, England
- 1969-1971 Star Performer, "Holiday on Ice" show in Europe and North America
- Command Performance for Queen of England, Premier of Russia, and Charlie Chaplin
- Coached and helped Scott Hamilton, Dorothy Hamill, Elvis Stojko, Rudy Galindo, Tai Babilonia, Randy Gardner, Sasha Cohen, Luc Robitaille, Doug Smith, Robert Mendel, Angela Ruggiero, Jerry Bruckheimer, Bruce Jenner, Mayor Richard Riordan, Architect Frank Gehry, Actress Lynn Holly Johnson and Winona Ryder, and actors like Mike Myers, Jim Carrey, Rob Lowe, Arnold Schwarzenegger and many, many more
- Producer of "Legends on Ice," Las Vegas, Nevada, and Atlantic City, New Jersey
- Founder and CEO of United Fitness Foundation
- Presidentially-appointed member of the President's Council on Physical Fitness (along with Arnold Schwarzenegger)
- Five-time president of Southern Californian Olympians
- Advisor, California Governor's Fitness Council

- Advisor, Board of Directors, Professional Skaters Guild of America
- Ed Sullivan Show guest performer
- CBS Commentator
- Director of Choreography, Trapper John M.D., ice skating episode
- Director of Choreography – Ice Castles major motion picture
- Vice president of Gala Entertainment Ice Show Company
- Co-founder of "Bring Hollywood Home Foundation" in 2009, a 501c4

International, World & Olympic Competitive Students
I have had the pleasure of coaching ...

Tai Babalonia and Randy Gardner (USA)

Jean Yun (Korea)

David Delposo (Mexico)

Tina Washington (India)

Trifun Zivanovic (USA and Serbia)

Hoy Sun Kim (Korea)

Peter and Elizabeth Cain (Australia)

Belinda Kothard (Australia)

Robin Burley (Australia)

Michael Amentez (Australia)

Ksenija Jastenjski (Serbia)

Sasha Cohen (USA)

Taka Kozuka (Japan)

And some 15 other U.S. National Competitors ...

Gary has also coached at over 500 competitions, 35 international
competitions, 20 U.S. National Championships, 18 World
Championships, and five Olympic Games

A salute to a few of my friends gone too early...

1. The entire 1961 U.S. Figure Skating Team, judges, and friends
2. Don McPherson
3. Tim Brown
4. Dean Paul Martin Jr.
5. Doug Ramsey
6. Andrea Nepela
7. Steve Box
8. Monty Hoyt
9. Peter Kollen
10. John Curry
11. Ronnie Robertson
12. Anna Galmarini
13. Guy Riville
14. Tommy Miller
15. Paul McGrath
16. Hana Maskovia
17. Dwayne Mackie
18. Jimmie Desbrow
19. Robert Wagenhoffer
20. Ray Balmer
21. Billy Chapel
22. Christopher Bowman
23. Carlo Fassi
24. Scott Daniels
25. Mr. P. Brunet
26. Mr. Don Stewart

27. Debby Visconti, my sister gone May 13, 2014, to whom I dedicate eternal friendship

Made in the USA
Middletown, DE
16 July 2015